Verona, Italy

Travel and Tourism

Author
Aaron Ellis.

Publisher:
SONITTEC LTD
College House, 2nd
Floor
17 King Edwards
Road,
Ruislip
London
HA4 7AE.

Table of Content

Summary

Traveling Values

Verona Travel: There are plenty of things one can gain from exploring different places such as new friends, new experiences and new stories. When you start exploring new places, you get a better understanding of the people living there including their culture, history and background.

Studies show that travelling can improve your overall health and enhance your creativity. Therefore, you need to take time out from your daily tasks, office responsibilities, hectic schedule and everyday pressures at least once in a year. Plan a tour to a new city with an open schedule and let life present you with the numerous opportunities that are waiting for you.

- ✓ Improves Social and Communication Skills

- ✓ Ensures Peace of Mind

- ✓ Helps you Get Original and Creative Thoughts

- ✓ Broadens Your Horizons

- ✓ Enhances your Tolerance for Uncertainty

- ✓ Boosts Up your Confidence:

- ✓ Gets you Real-life Education

- ✓ Creates Memories for Lifetime

- ✓ Creates Memories for Lifetime

- ✓ Helps you Have Fun

- ✓ Aids you Get to Know Yourself

One of the main benefits of travelling, especially to areas where your native language is not widely used, is that you learn how to communicate with all manner of different people. It could be communicating to find the way to your next destination or asking for the nearest restaurant.

We all have stress and tension in our lives. Traveling forces us to temporarily disconnect from our normal routine and it helps us appreciate the people and things you have around. As per a famous saying "we never know what we have until we lose it."

It is believed that if someone gets out of their comfort zone, the mind gets more creative. To develop new neural connections that trigger original and creative thoughts, you must explore new places and break out of your daily lifestyles.

Travelling helps you connect with different people from different cultures, and this is fatal to prejudice, bigotry and narrow-mindedness. Meeting people from different cultures and societies will help you see issues and daily life from many different angles.

While travelling, you will find yourself stuck in situations where things don't always go as planned. Such situations will help you learn to cope with the uncertainties in life.

Being in a place where you do not know anyone will assist you to gain confidence and presence of mind. You will develop the ability to cope with obstacles, which will make you a confident person and help you grow as a person.

Meeting different people from vast cultures and societies provides an education that is impossible to get in a traditional school, college or a university. There is no substitute for the real thing.

If you travel with friends and family members, traveling helps you build stronger bonds and make memories. You can also save memories of a lifetime by creating photo albums or sharing photos in social media

No matter how young or old you are, no matter your profession, there is always a time when the child in you wants to have some fun. When you travel, you do not care what you do at all and you can just break free from the norm.

While traveling, you might find yourself stuck in situations you would not ordinary experience in your daily life. Such a situation can help you understand yourself and how you react to such circumstances and prepare you for future similar situations.

Although traveling offers many benefits, it also has some disadvantages if not planned carefully.

If you are a patient and taking medication for a disease, do not forget to carry your medication. Keeping jet lag pills handy saves you from unnecessary discomfort.

Those susceptible to allergies should carry allergy medication. Plan your tour in advance, prepare a checklist to keep yourself healthy while traveling and pack important items before you travel.

Travelling is good for the health so decide a place now and pack your bags. Remember, you only live once, so start traveling to different places and get some life-altering experiences.

Introduction

It's the setting of the world's greatest love story, but Verona has more to offer than just Romeo and Juliet. While romance, conflict and passion shaped the city, it's the Roman, medieval and Renaissance architects that earned it UNESCO World Heritage status.

Verona's remarkably well-preserved architecture is crowned by its magnificent amphitheatre, the Arena, which has remained intact for two centuries. 25,000 spectators still take to its marble seats during Verona's summer opera festival.

Known as piccolo Roma (little Rome), Verona's narrow streets are a rich collection of beautiful buildings and baroque facades. With its stunning historic monuments, wide variety of restaurants and fabulous shopping, Verona has all the ingredients for the perfect weekend break.

Roman gates, sections of the original city wall and other ruins are found at every turn. The elegant, three-storey Porta rises wonderfully above Corso Porta Borsari, the city's best shopping street.

Still, it's Romeo and Juliet who have left the greatest mark. Discover the amour and agony of devotion at the 14th-century balcony of Casa di Giulietta, where lovers graffiti hopeful pleas on the courtyard walls.

Romeo's banishment took place in the magnificent Cortile del Mercato Vecchio, while the tale's epilogue leads visitors to Juliet's tomb in the crypt of San Francisco al Corso monastery.

Verona has more than its fair share of beautiful churches. With elegant rounded arches and soft yellow stone, the magnificent Basilica of San Zeno Maggiore is regarded as one of the finest Romanesque buildings in the world.

Rising above the whole city is Castelvecchio, the ancient castle which overlooks the surrounding Valpolicella and Soave wine districts. But little beats striding along the Via Mazzoni to peek into its boutique shops and designer chains, or visiting the buzzing market stalls on Piazza delle Erbe.

Situated in the affluent and culturally rich Veneto region of north eastern Italy, Verona is within a few hours train ride or car journey from Venice, Vicenza and Padua, so works well as a base from which to explore this particularly beautiful and historic part of the country.

History

Verona city was founded by an ancient tribe (possibly the Euganei or Raeti) and was later occupied by the Gallic Cenomani. It became a Roman colony in 89 BCE and rapidly rose in importance because it was at the junction of main roads between Italy and northern Europe. The poet Catullus was born there. Verona was occupied by the Ostrogoth king Theodoric (489), who built a castle on the site of the present Castel San Pietro on the Adige River. The city remained important under the Lombard kings. It was captured by Charlemagne in 774 and was the residence of his son Pippin and of Berengar of Tours.

Verona was an independent commune from the early 12th century, and it suffered during the early struggles between the Guelfs (papal party) and Ghibellines (imperial party), in the course of which it chose the Guelf party. Ruled by the tyrant Ezzelino da Romano (1226–59), the city grew calmer and prospered under the della Scala (Scaliger) family after Mastino I della Scala became podesta (chief magistrate) in 1260. In the reign of Bartolomeo della Scala, Romeo Montague and Juliet Capulet traditionally loved and died; their romance is commemorated by the so-called Tomb of Juliet, Romeo's House, and Juliet's House. Bartolomeo's brother Cangrande I (died 1329), the greatest member of the della Scala family, protected the exiled poet Dante. Verona fell to Gian Galeazzo Visconti in 1387 and in 1405 to Venice, which held it, apart from its occupation by Emperor Maximilian I (1509–17), until 1797, when it was ceded to Austria by Napoleon I at the Treaty of Campo Formio. The last congress of the Quadruple Alliance (Russia, Prussia, Austria, Britain) was held at Verona in 1822. In 1866 the city was united to the Kingdom of Italy. It suffered heavy damage in World War II but has since been restored.

Verona is one of the richest cities in northern Italy in Roman remains. The most remarkable of these, the amphitheatre, or Arena, is the third largest surviving Roman amphitheatre and is now used for opera. Also from the 1st century CE are the Roman theatre (with adjacent archaeological museum) and two gateways. The Arco dei Gavi (reconstructed in 1932) was erected in the 1st century BCE. The Lapidario Maffeiano Museum (1714) contains Greek and Roman antiquities.

Verona is remarkable for its rich Romanesque and Gothic architecture, which is often in a distinctive pink brick.

The city produced two great Renaissance architects, Fra Giocondo and Michele Sanmicheli. Its outstanding churches include the Romanesque San Zeno Maggiore (originally 5th century, rebuilt 1117–1227), with a brick and marble facade, a celebrated marble porch, and a triptych by the 14th-century painter Andrea Mantegna, and the Gothic Sant'Anastasia (foundation 1290; completed 1422–81). The Romanesque-Gothic cathedral (rebuilt 15th century) contains an Assumption by the 16th-century artist Titian and one of Europe's oldest libraries. Also notable are the churches of San Fermo Maggiore, comprising two 11th-century edifices, the upper rebuilt after 1313; SS.

Nazzaro and Celso, rebuilt in 1464–83; and San Giorgio in Braida, begun in 1477 and consecrated in 1536, partially designed by Sanmicheli. Notable secular landmarks include the Castelvecchio (now the Civic Museum, Verona), built by Cangrande II in 1354; the Loggia del Consiglio (1493), attributed to Fra Giocondo; the Arche Scaligere, comprising the elaborate Scaliger tombs with Gothic canopies surmounted by equestrian statues; the Palazzo della Ragione (1193; much altered); and the Ponte Scaligero (1354), rebuilt after being damaged in World War II.

Verona was also a renowned medieval centre of painting. The work of Antonio Pisanello (Pisano) climaxes the courtly fresco work of the 14th and 15th centuries. The influence of Bartolommeo Montagna of Vicenza and his father-in-law, the Venetian Jacopo Bellini, in the 15th century combined with that of Venice to affect the whole Veronese school. The city's most famous painter was the 15th-century artist Paolo Caliari (Paolo Veronese), who spent most of his active life in Venice although his Martyrdom of St. George remains in San Giorgio in Braida at Verona.

The city is the centre of rail and road connections from northern Italy to central Europe via the Brenner Pass; it links Milan and Venice by rail and road and is served by airports at Boscomantico and Villafranca. Verona ships fruits and vegetables to central Europe and is noted for its cereal market and its annual International Agricultural and Horse Fair (since 1898). There are engineering, chemical, and paper industries, sugar refining, and diversified manufactures. Artistic furniture making and work in precious metals and marble are flourishing handicraft industries, and Verona's traditional wines

(Amarone, Bardolino, Valpolicella, Soave, and Recioto) are famous. Pop. (2011 est.) mun., 254,607.

Tourism

Many travelers associate the charming Italian city of Verona with the romantic love story of Romeo and Juliet. This picturesque place with a rich history is a UNESCO World Heritage Site. Every year, it is visited by more than three million tourists. The city is famous not only for its priceless historical and architectural monuments, but also for a rich cultural life. There are joyful festivals and exhibitions all year round.

Verona has numerous unique monuments of Ancient Rome. The undisputed symbol of the city is the Arena di Verona, as well as the beautiful Roman theater and Gavi Arch. Numerous gothic churches and gorgeous palaces are reminiscent of the era of the Middle Ages. One of the most visited sites is associated with the names from the famous Shakespeare play. Despite the fact that the story of Romeo and Juliet is a fiction, many romantic natures still tend to see houses of lovers and visit the tomb of Juliet and other significant places of Verona, which appear in the play one way or another.

Fans of museums won't be bored in Verona, too. The Archaeological Museum is one of the most interesting and most visited in the city. As noted earlier, the whole area of Verona and its surroundings is an important archaeological area where a lot of priceless artifacts dating back to ancient Greece and Rome were found. Romantic Verona with its picturesque canals and pedestrian bridges is perfect for walking and a relaxing holiday. This city without doubt is one of the most amazing in the world.

Sightseeing in Verona

What to see. Complete travel guide

Verona is a cozy provincial town that is also known as the home of Shakespeare's Romeo and Juliet. In terms of the number of sights and architectural heritage Verona is a worthy competitor to Milan and Rome.

Ancient Roman Amphitheater is known as the most famous sight of Verona. It was built yet in the 1st century AD. Moreover, the amphitheater is working and this is the most famous opera theater in the town. Every art connoisseur should definitely visit live performances that take place there for more than a century. You can also see many architectural sights near Piazza delle Erbe. Here you will find an ancient Domus Mercatorum house built in the gothic style and the local town hall. In ancient times the Roman Forum was located on the territory of the square, while Domus Mercatorum was the residence of guilds. Palazzo Vescovile is also a noble architectural building. Built in the 15th century, this palace features 5 statues installed on cornice. The statues show famous people of that time that made a serious impact on Verona and its development.

While making a walk on the streets of Verona, you will see numerous ancient churches and cathedrals on your way. One of the biggest and most famous of them is Santa Maria Antica Church. St. Anastasia Church is also known as the most beautiful building. Its floor is decorated with mosaics made of pink, white and blue marble, and the church's walls feature magnificent frescos. The halls of the church store pictures of local artists, so this excursion will be very interesting for people who like art.

The local Cathedral can be called an example of the architecture of Verona. Built in the 12th century, this building amazes its visitors by rich decorations of halls, which luxurious design is made with rare red marble, gilding and fine murals. The mentioned places are just a small share of sights you can see in Verona. Tourists from all over the world traditionally find much interesting here.

The most romantic site in Verona is the House of Juliet - a beautiful historic building of the 13th century, located on Via Cappello. It was in this house, according to Shakespeare's history, that the family of the Capulets lived. Today in the courtyard of the historic building, there is a sculpture of Juliet. In the building itself, which is the most valuable architectural monument today, there is an interesting museum devoted to Shakespearean characters. This attraction is most often visited by couples in love. They all want to be photographed under the balcony of Juliet, and also leave a note on the wall of the historic building, on which is written a cherished desire.

In Verona, there is also the House of Romeo - a strict building in the medieval style, which was built in the 14th century. According to available historical data, this building has never belonged to the family of Montagues, but admirers of the Shakespearean tragedy still consider it a matter of honor to visit this literary landmark. Currently, the spectacular medieval building is in private ownership, so it will not be possible to admire its interior decoration.

Among the outstanding architectural sights, the Palazzo Maffei should definitely be distinguished. Its construction began in the 15th century, and it was completed only 200 years later. Today, this palace is considered a true masterpiece of baroque architecture. Its facade is adorned with skilful statues of Roman gods, graceful arches and balconies. In the immediate vicinity of the palace is the ancient clock tower Gardello, which was erected as far back as the 15th century. They are usually regarded as a single architectural ensemble.

Travelers who dream of walking around the territory of real ancient castle should go to Castelvecchio. This castle on the banks of the Adige River was built in the middle of the 14th century. For many years, it stood guard over the tranquility of the city. Today in the majestic castle is a very interesting museum with a diverse collection. A collection of weapons, priceless works of art, as well as ancient jewelry can also be seen. Dozens of unique historical and religious monuments are preserved on the territory of Verona. In addition, many unique museums and art galleries operate in the city.

Arena di Verona

The Roman amphitheatre in Verona

After the Colosseum in Rome and the amphitheatre in Capua, the Roman arena in Verona is the third largest Roman amphitheatre. With its gigantic dimensions of 140 metres in length and 110 metres in width it dominates the Piazza Brà from the north. Its great acoustics and unique location make the Roman arena the ideal location for events and it attracts hundreds of thousands of visitors to Verona every year during the Festival season to see the opera and theatre performances.

Arena di Verona: A long history of success

The arena in Verona was built in the 1st century AD by the Flavian emperors according to the principle of "bread and games". For almost 400 years gladiators fought here and entertained the masses with bloody carnage. When emperor Honorius prohibited the gladiator games in 404 AD, that was the end of the Arena of Verona and the amphitheatre stood empty for centuries. The original four-floor building with a length of 152 metres and a width of 113 metres was damaged in the 12th century by several earthquakes and reduced to its present size the interior zone. The four-floor exterior the remains are only three stories tall with 4 arches still gives a good impression of the glory of the former curtain wall surrounded by columns.

On account of its dark catacombs, the Roman arena was often called the "labyrinth of the devil" by the Veronese people and was primarily used as a quarry for the surrounding residential buildings. The first to return to their roots in the Renaissance, the Venetians restored the venerable walls. Since then, sporadic concerts, bullfights and theatrical performances have been held in the arena once more.

Arena di Verona: A perfect opera experience

There has been a real boom in the Roman Arena in Verona since 1913. On the occasion of Giuseppe Verdi's birthday the Verona opera festival was inaugurated and has inspired visitors to the 22,000-seat arena since then. From June to August you can admire an event almost every day, and if you have the chance to see one of the great performances you should definitely do it. Short-break visitors also have the chance to purchase a ticket for unnumbered seats for less than 30 euros at the box office turning up in the morning on time is required. If you have a prior booking and show up in appropriate evening attire you can also buy some of the expensive seat tickets in the stalls.

Basilica di San Zeno

Basilica di San Zeno Maggiore
One of the most beautiful Romanesque basilicas in Italy
The Basilica di San Zeno Maggiore is one of the most beautiful Romanesque basilicas in Italy. It was created under the direction of Pippin, son of Charlemagne, on the ruins of an ancient Benedictine monastery. It is dedicated to the former Bishop and patron saint of Verona, San

Zeno. The basilica was completed in 1138, and on its outer façade you can see Veronese engineering typical for the period, which mixed different coloured building materials. Under the beautiful rose window you enter the basilica through a bronze door which is framed with magnificent reliefs by the Master Nicolò which immortalise a number of famous scenes from Genesis and the Bible.

The outdoor area of the basilica includes a beautiful Romanesque bell tower and a crenelated defence tower. The adjoining cloister is supported by double columns and contains many graves.

The interior of San Zeno Maggiore

If you enter the three-aisled basilica, the eye is immediately drawn to the impressive chorus of the crypt. You can reach the high church and choir via a staircase that is located in the nave. Left and right of the main entrance are two baptismal fonts whose sandstone basin dates from the second century and was originally located in a Roman bath house. The highlight of the Basilica di San Zeno Maggiore is the famous triptych in the main Gothic chapel. It was created by Andrea Mantegna in 1459 and shows Maria. It is surely one of the masterpieces of Northern Italian Renaissance. Many other paintings were looted by Napoleon and can be admired in the Louvre in Paris today.

You can find the most important fresco in the north-western part of the church, "The Crucifixion" by Altichiero from the 14th century. Just behind the high altar on the left-hand side in the apse you can see the smiling statue of Saint San Zeno. It is made of black marble, which symbolises the supposed the saint's supposed

African origins. San Zeno's sarcophagus is in the open crypt. The crypt appears to the visitor like a huge portico and it contains many old frescoes and a modern painting of the crucifixion.

Torre dei Lamberti

Palazzo del Comune with Torre dei Lamberti
Great view over Verona

A special attraction in Verona, besides the Roman arena, is the Palazzo del Comune with its looming Torre dei Lamberti. You can enjoy the best view over Verona from the tower and get a good impression of the position and appearance of the city. Right next to the tower you can reach the Piazza dei Signori through the Arco della Costa.

Palazzo del Comune the oldest city hall in Italy

The Palazzo del Comune, also called Palazzo della Ragione, was probably built in 1193 and is the oldest city hall in Italy. Originally the construction included four massive towers of which only the Torre dei Lamberti and a stump of a second tower remain. Three major fires in 1218, 1541 and 1723 destroyed large parts of the building, including the towers. After several modifications, the palace reached its present form. The magnificent neo-classical façade facing the Piazza delle Erbe was preserved, while at the rear of the palace at the Piazza dei Signori it appears in a Renaissance style.

The Palazzo del Comune was the seat of the government of Verona the great council of the city met regularly in the big hall on the first floor. In the large courtyard with the beautiful staircase there was originally a market this is where the performances of the Verona Summer Theatre Festival take place today. Tickets and information can be found at www.estateteatraleveronese.it.

Occasional art exhibitions have been held at the palace since 2007.

View from the Torre dei Lamberti

The 83-metre-high Torre dei Lamberti was built in 1172 and was the only tower in Verona that belonged to the Lamberti family. In 1464 the octagonal tower floor with its two bells "Rengo" and "Marangona" was added to the basement. The "Rengo" bell called the people to arms in case of an attack, while the "Marangona" ball announced the end of a working day or a fire in the city.

You can enjoy a beautiful view over Verona from the observation deck of the tower. The top can be reached either by lift or by climbing 368 arduous steps. In fine weather you will also have a nice view over the surrounding hills.

Cathedral of Verona

Duomo Santa Maria Matricolare
Verona Cathedral

Verona's cathedral, the Duomo Santa Maria Matricolare, is a fantastic mix of Romanesque and Gothic elements. The typical Veronese strip design from two different building materials is already apparent from the exterior. The cathedral itself dates from the 8th century. Prior to this there was a small basilica on the same site, which was replaced by the cathedral after it was destroyed by an earthquake. The new cathedral was called the "Mother Church" Santa Maria Marticolare. Numerous modifications and constructions explain the cathedral's current appearance. Particularly noteworthy is the facade portal by Master Nicolò with two beautiful bas-reliefs. In the 15th century the cathedral was reconstructed in neo-Gothic style.

The gleaming white tower was completed in the 20th century.

Inside the cathedral

The Duomo Santa Maria Matricolare is a three-aisled church with richly decorated aisles and numerous chapels. Well worth seeing is the first chapel to the left, the Capella Nichesola, with its famous altarpiece "Assumption" by Titian. The picture shows the apostles kneeling around Mary's coffin and the mother of god herself floating in towering clouds. The kneeling and praying apostle to the left represents the artist Sanmicheli.

Also worth seeing is the main work by Liberale di Verona "Adoration of the Magi" in the second chapel to the right. The Capella Mazzanti houses the sarcophagus of St. Agatha. The sarcophagus was made in the style of the Scaliger in the 14th century and shows the saint as she protects the poor, pastoralists, goldsmiths and weavers from breast diseases, animal diseases and earthquakes. You can enter the baptistery of San Giovanni through an inconspicuous door to the left of the apse. Worth seeing here is the octagonal font, which was carved from a single block of marble. Several metres from the baptistery you will find the small chapel of Saint Helen, which features a number of Roman floor mosaics.

Castelvecchio

Fortress of the Scaliger

This large medieval brick castle was built in 1354 by the Scaliger Cangrande II and is one of Europe's most important art centres. An enclosure wall surrounds the castle battlements and its 6 towers. In the Middle Ages the outer wall was protected by a moat. Contrary to all speculation, the fortress was not built to defend against enemies from without but against the Veronese people who hated the dynasty of the Scala family. The City Palace at the Piazza dei Signori was abandoned and the noble family moved to the Castelvecchio. Ironically, the inward-looking fortress was finally conquered from without when the Milanese Visconti put an end to the rule of the Scaliger in Verona.

After the Lords of Verona, the Venetians, French and Austrians used the fortress before it was restored in 1923 and opened as a museum in 1925.

The Museo di Castelvecchio

You can reach the residence of the Scala family, which now houses the Museo Civico d'Arte, by crossing the courtyard. The museum houses one of the most important art collections in Europe. In room 1 the sarcophagus of St. Sergius and Bacchus from 1179 deserves special attention. Further highlights in the other rooms include the portrait of the child by Francesco Caroto (1480-1555), one of the most famous paintings in the museum, and the altar by Turine dei Maxio (1356-1387).

Numerous paintings from the Veronese and Venetian school can be found in room 14. Among these are paintings of Stefano di Verona ("Virgin and child"), Pisanello ("Madonna with the Quail"), Jacobo Bellini ("Madonna of Humility") and Andrea Mantega ("The Holy Family with St. Julia"). Another impressive piece is the original statue from the grave of Cangrande I from the Tombs of the Scaliger.

Given the wealth of exhibits to see, you should definitely take a few hours to visit the museum and the fortress properly. Visitors who are not so interested in art can walk around the courtyard of the castle and get a good impression of fortress's erstwhile might.

Chiesa Santa Anastasia

The largest church in Verona

The church of St. Anastasia is the largest church in Verona. The massive Gothic brick building was built by the Dominicans between the 13th and the 15th century. Originally two churches built by King Theoderic, the churches of Anastasius and Remigio were located here. In 1261 both churches were taken over by the Dominicans and developed over two centuries of work into a single mighty church. Although the impressive façade was never completed, the new Chiesa Sant'Anastasia was dedicated in 1481.

Inside the Chiesa Sant'Anastasia

The church of Santa Anastasia is a perfect example of the Italian-dominated Gothic style. The interior of the church is dark and the high cross-ribbed vault is supported by massive circular columns. By the first columns you can see two dwarfs popularly known as "the hunchbacks" bending under the weight of two fonts. The three-nave church is divided by a transept just in front of the altar. Six chapels are located at the ends of the transept. Six richly decorated altars with pictures and illustrations by famous artists such as Danese Cataneo, Sanmicheli, Liberale da Verona and Francesco Caroto decorate the right-hand nave and the side wall of the transept.

The chapels and frescoes of the Chiesa Sant'Anastasia

Set slightly further back, the chapel of the crucifixion represents the oldest part of the church of St. Anastasia and marks the place where the small church's eponymous predecessor once stood. The portrait of the crucifixion dates from the 15th century and the tomb on the left-hand side is by Giansello da Folgaria. In the next chapel, the Cavalli chapel, you can admire the church's first highlight, the beautiful fresco of "Madonna with three saints and the Cavalli family" by Altichiero. It was created in 1375 and depicts three noble knights who entrust three members of the Cavalli family to the mother of God.

The Pellegrini chapel just next door attracts attention mainly on account of its entirely brickwork construction. In the main chapel in the centre you can see the tomb of the Scaliger commander Cortesia Serego on the left-hand side and the great fresco "The last judgement" by Turone on the right-hand wall of the choir.

Cappella Giusti

The most famous fresco of the Chiesa Sant'Anastasia is located in the Capella Giusti in the left-hand transept. It was here that Antonio Pisanello (1380-1455) painted the fresco "Departure of St. George to fight the dragon". It is considered to be the high point and at the same time the end point of the Gothic style in northern Italy. It shows Saint George, who is jumping into the saddle to save the beautiful princess from the dragon. Although it is still in the high Gothic tradition, the fresco already shows first signs of the early Renaissance with strong foreshortening and an unusual depth for this period, which you can explore best by looking at the horse.

Cappella San Pietro Martire

If you leave the Chiesa Sant'Anastasia through the main entrance, you can see the Gothic tomb of the nobleman Castelbarco just left over the gate. The small chapel of San Pietro Martire (also called Cappella San Giorgetto) is located right next to the tomb. It is dedicated to Saint Peter of Verona and contains some beautiful frescoes.

Juliet's house

Location of Shakespeare's play

Juliet's house (Casa di Giulietta) is one of the main attractions of Verona with the most famous balcony in the world. Every day crowds of people make their way through the narrow archway into the courtyard to admire and photograph the famous balcony. Couples of all ages swear eternal fidelity here in memory of Shakespeare's play "Romeo and Juliet".

And all this even though the two main characters never really existed and William Shakespeare never went to Verona in his lifetime. However, Verona is inextricably linked with the fate of the two lovers. In recognition of this factor and in order to offer the countless couples who come to Verona every year a worthy location, the city of Verona bought today's house of Juliet from the Dal Capello family in 1905. Due to the similarity of their names they declared the house to be the family residence of the Capuleti family a new tourist sensation was created!

In the footsteps of Romeo and Juliet

Those who enter the courtyard of Juliet's house for the first time will be struck by the thousands of small scraps of paper which cover the floor to the ceiling. All who write down their love vows to their partner and stick them on the wall will according to the popular belief stay together with their partner for the rest of their lives and will be very happy. Even touching the right breast of the bronze statue of Juliet in the small courtyard will bring luck to all who are trying to find their true love.

Apart from the famous love story, Juliet's house has other interesting attractions to offer. The house delights with its beautiful Gothic style from the 14th century. In the individual rooms and halls you can find numerous exhibits from the time of Romeo and Juliet which give a good impression of life in ancient Verona.

Piazza Brà

Main square and bustling centre of Verona

Verona's main square, the Piazza Brà, is one of the largest squares in Europe. It functions as a kind of arrival hall before you enter the centre of the city. The term "brà" derives originally from the German word "breit" (broad) and refers to the broad square in front of the city gates. Even today, the Piazza Brà is a beautiful and wide square in the heart of Verona with many open spaces and cosy street bars. Many historic buildings from various eras from ancient times to the present surround the square. From your coffee table in one of the bars you can thus enjoy 2,000 years of history at a glance.

Piazza Brà: 2,000 years of Veronese history

Restaurants, magnificent palaces and buildings dating back over 2,000 years surround the Piazza Brà in Verona. In the north, the impressive Roman amphitheatre rises high above the square. The Portoni del Brà archway and parts of the medieval city wall enclose the square to the south. Directly by the city walls you will see the neo-classical Palazzo Gran Guardia and the Museo Lapidario Maffeiano archaeological museum. To the southeast of the square is the Palazzo Municipale (also called Palazzo Barbieri), Verona's town hall, which was built in 1840 by the Austrians. From its steps you can enjoy great views over the Piazza Brà.

Attractions at the Piazza Brà

The promenade on the Piazza Brà itself is paved with pink marble from the Valpolicella region. The centre of the spacious square is dominated by an equestrian statue of the Italian King Vittorio Emanuele II (1820 - 1878). The statue of the first ruler of the united Italy was unveiled on

9th January 1883, the 5th anniversary of the death of the king.

The fountain in the park, the Fonatna delle Alpi or Münchner-Kindlbrunnen, was constructed on the occasion of Verona's twinning with Munich and was sponsored by the Germans. In return a statue of Juliet was erected at the Old Town Hall in Munich. The people of Verona often refer jokingly to the fountain as the "Lemon Squeezer" (struca limoni) because it looks like one with its shape. Also a result of the twinning is a memorial for the displaced Italians into German concentration camps, which is under the trees at Piazza Brà.

The Piazza Brà is still one of the busiest places in Verona with many nice restaurants and street cafes. If you have enough time, you should certainly stay here for a while and enjoy the impressions of this beautiful and historic place.

Piazza delle Erbe

Lively heart of Verona

The Piazza delle Erbe has remained the vibrant heart of Verona. Many restaurants have their tables and chairs on the streets and market stalls, which offer mainly souvenirs but also fruits and vegetables, are set up in the middle of the square every day. The Piazza delle Erbe was also the central square in Roman times the forum romanum which played host to Verona's political, economic and social life.

Many magnificent buildings, including the baroque Palazzo Maffei and the Case dei Mazzanti with its beautiful frescoes inside, surround the square. The Torre del Gardello a clock tower which was built in 1370 by the

Scaliger Cansignorio is located right next to the Palazzo Maffei. In 1421 a clock face was added to the bell tower to show the citizens the correct time. The winged lion in front of the Palazzo, the Colonia di San Marco, was erected by the Venetians and served as a symbol of Venice's might.

Other sights at the Piazza delle Erbe

In the middle of the square you can see a small raised canopy from the 16th century. It was here that the market surveillance, which had a good view over the square, was located. Anyone who was found guilty of cheating was chained to the Tribune and had to expose himself to the ridicule of the people. New laws and announcements were also published at the Tribuna.

An eye-catcher is the beautiful fountain "Fontana dei Madonna Verona". In the middle of the fountain is a Madonna sculpture with a banner that celebrates the beauty of Verona. Another remarkable sight is the Colonna del Mercato, a beautiful Gothic market column, which was built by Visconti in 1401. The bronze sculpture next to it depicts the Veronese poet Roberto Tiberio Barbarani (1872–1945)

At the southwest edge of the square, in front of the Torre dei Lamberti and the Palazzo del Commune, from which you have the best view over Verona, you can find the Casa dei Mercanti. The merchants house was built in 1301 by the lords of Verona, and with its crenelated façade it is still an eye-catcher at the Piazza delle Erbe.

Piazza dei Signori

Verona's centre of power
The Piazza dei Signori was the former centre of power in Verona. Around the beautiful square all

important main buildings of the former city government, including the court and the seat of power of the Scaliger family, are located. A large statue by the famous Italian poet Dante Alighieri has dominated the square since 1865 and gave the square the nickname "Piazza Dante".

Loggia del Consiglio the most magnificent building at the Piazza dei Signori

Diagonally opposite the Palazzo del Comune, on the other side of the square, you can see the Loggia del Consiglio one of the square's most magnificent buildings. It was built in 1476 by Fra Giocondo and is a masterpiece of the Venetian Renaissance and unique in Verona. The beautiful façade with its columned double windows and statues on the roof shine through the pastel colours of the walls even more impressively. The statues of Alberto da Milano imitate famous

Italians who are thought to have been born in Verona: Gaius Valerius Catullus, Pliny the Elder, Aemilius Macer, Marcus Vitruvius Pollio and Cornelius Nepos.

Palazzo del Podestà, Arco della Tortura and Casa della Pièta

To the left of the Loggia you will find the Casa della Pièta, a simple Renaissance building whose special feature is a bas-relief on the façade. It shows a seated woman with a flag the symbol of the city of Verona during the rule of Venice.

The Palazzo del Podestà, also called Palazzo del Governo, right next to the Loggia del Consiglio was once the seat of power of the Scaliger family. Unfortunately, the magnificent frescoes by Giotto di Bondone no longer exist today you can only see some fragments of the frescoes in the courtyard. The Arco della Tortura, so named because the torture instruments of the Veronese judges hung here, connects the Palazzo del Podestà with the Palazzo dei Tribunali.

Palazzo Tribunali and Palazzo dei Giudici

The Palazzo dei Tribunali (the court) is connected by an arch to the Palazzo del Comune and dates from 1575. The Porta Bombardiera, decorated with two cannons in the palace courtyard, is worth a visit. In the courtyard you will also find excavations of the Roman foundations with parts of a mosaic floor. The last palace is the Palazzo dei Giudici at the top end of the Piazza dei Signori. The court of Verona has been based here since 1731.

Ponte Scaligero

Escape-bridge of the Scaliger

At an impressive length of more than 120 metres, the Ponte Scaligero leads from the

Castelvecchio over the Adige. Two solid foundations carry the columns of the bridge's three large arches. The castellated bridge has a very clear defensive character. But, like the Castelvecchio, it was not built for defensive purposes against an enemy from without but served only as an escape route for the hated Scaliger family in the case of a popular uprising. The members of the noble family hoped that it would provide a safe escape route over the river and a successful flight into the Adige Valley.

During World War II the bridge was blown up by German soldiers and rebuilt in 1951 using the original parts, which were lying around in the river. Today the bridge is open for everyone and connects the old town with the opposite bank of the Adige river. Many local people and numerous passers-by enjoy the view over the city from here.

Scaliger Tombs

The Scavi Scaligeri tombs of the lords of Verona

With their very finest stone-carved sarcophagi, the Scala family's tombs are among the most famous photographic motifs of the city of Verona. High above the entrance of the family church of the Scala family, the Chiesa Santa Maria Antica, the tomb of the most important Scaliger, Cangrande I (1291-1329), reigns supreme. In allusion to his epithet "Big Dog", four dogs support the sarcophagus onto which the portrait of Cangrande is carved. The sarcophagus is protected by a large canopy topped by an imposing equestrian statue. The original statue can be admired in the Castelvecchio.

The Scaliger family's peak: Mastino II and Cansignorio

The rest of the graves are fenced off and, unfortunately, can only be viewed from outside. Noteworthy among these are the tombs of Mastino II (1308-1351) and his son Cansignorio (1334-1375) under whom the rule of the Scaliger reached its peak. The grave of Mastino, the mastiff, is surrounded by marble and ornate wrought-iron ladders (ladder = Scala, the heraldic symbol of the Scaliger). It rests on four pillars, creating the structure of a crown with a turret. Mastino himself is riding in full armour on the turret.

While it is the most richly decorated, the grave of Cansignorio, the lead dog, is considered to be the least artistically valuable tomb. Six knights in tabernacles guard his tomb. Cansignorio himself is also shown at atop his horse the quality of his statue cannot compete with those of his predecessors.

More tombs of the Scaliger

In addition to these three famous Scaliger lords you will also find the tombs of Mastino I, Alberto I, Bartolomeo I, Cangrande II and Bartolomeo II. The church of Santa Maria Antica, the family church of the Scala family, is a beautiful example of Veronese Romanesque architecture. The use of two different building materials, which are used in strip-shaped turns, is especially typical of the Veronese architectural style. The interior of the church was revised and restored several times in the central nave you can find some frescoes from the early 14th century.

Castel San Pietro

Austrian fort overlooking Verona

Directly above the Roman theatre you can find the Castel San Pietro splendid barracks from the Austrian period. You can reach the Castel by taking the stairs right next to the Teatro Romano. The fortress high above the city has been undergoing renovation works for several years to turn it into a museum and open it to visitors. Nevertheless, it is worthwhile visiting the Castel. In addition to the sight of the impressive building you will have a magnificent view over Verona from one of the terraces of the fortress. Another noteworthy feature of the fortifications are the five-square blocks, which were used by the Austrians to increase the stability of the fortress.

Ponte Pietra

Symbol of the history of Verona

The Ponte Pietra, formerly also known as "pons marmoreus" (marble bridge), is one of the oldest bridges in the city. At the foundation of Verona in 90 BC a wooden bridge crossed the Adige River here, which was replaced by a stone bridge by the Romans. In the Middle Ages the bridge was destroyed several times by floods and rebuilt time and again. Having been destroyed once again in the 16thcentury, the five-arch bridge seen today was built. The last time the Ponte Pietra was destroyed was in 1945 when German soldiers blew it up on their retreat. The bridge was restored to its former glory in 1959.

On the left bank downstream you can see the remains of the ancient arches of the old bridge. The two central arches of the Ponte Pietra, built of brick, are remnants from the Middle Ages. The bridge's eventful history and the preservation of elements from all periods, from ancient times to the present, have made the bridge a symbol of Verona's history.

Chiesa San Fermo Maggiore

Religious building with two churches in Verona

The Chiesa San Fermo Maggiore dates from the 5th century and houses the mortal remains of the martyrs San Fermo and San Rustco. The two Veronese men are buried in the main altar. In the 11th century the current Church of San Fermo was built here, a complete new church which includes the original building the original church is still open for visits today.

The exterior has the typical Veronese stripes design with two different colours of rock. Next to the main entrance you can see the tomb of Aventino Fracastoro, a Veronese physician. You can enter the church itself through the side portal.

Art in the Chiesa San Fermo Maggiore

An especially magnificent feature of the church's interior is the beautiful wooden ceiling, which extends over the entire nave. The two paintings of the crucifixion by Turrone and Altichieri over the main entrance and above the side entrance deserve special mention. Opposite the side portal you can still see some fragments of the fresco by Stefano da Verona, "Angels holding banners". In the right-hand corner to the back of the church is the mausoleum of Nicolò Brenzoni. The sculptor Nanni di Bartolo and the painter Pisanello created a masterpiece combining both sculpture and painting.

The lower church

To the right of the main altar you can reach the lower church of the Chiesa San Fermo Maggiore through a door. The lower church creates the impression of a multi-aisled construction because of its many pillars. On the walls and pillars you can still admire fragments of the frescoes from the 13th century.

Teatro Romano and Museo Archeologico

Roman theatre and archaeological museum

The Roman theatre was built in Verona at about the same time as the Roman arena. After the fall of Roman Empire, the Teatro Romano was, like the arena, used as a quarry and left to decay. The small church of San Siro e Libera still bears witness to the partial conversion of the theatre. You can still see 25 stone seats from the lower grandstand in the theatre. Besides a small loggia, unfortunately nothing remains of the multi-storey, figure-decorated front wall and the upper stand. Today the Teatro Romano is once again used for events. The Verona Summer Theatre

Festival attracts thousands of visitors to the theatre performances and concerts. More information and tickets can be found at www.estateteatraleveronese.it.

Archaeological museum with a magnificent city view

If you walk up the stairs along the rows of the Teatro Romano, you will arrive at the entrance to the archaeological museum, which is located within the walls of the old church. Inside you should pay particular attention to the beautiful mosaics and the Etruscan and Roman bronzes and sculptures. In the adjoining cloister you will see grave stones and inscriptions which date back to the date of the birth of Christ. Heading through the chapel you will reach the large terrace of the Museo Archeologico where you can enjoy a magnificent view over Verona.

Via Mazzini

Verona's largest pedestrian zone

The Via Mazzini forms a direct connection between the Piazza Brà and the Piazza delle Erbe. It is not only the largest pedestrian area of Verona, but is also one of the busiest streets of the city and Verona's shop window. Row upon row of shops line the road, and large crowds of tourists amble from window to window. All major Italian fashion brands are represented here and offer their goods. Anyone who is looking for the latest fashion in clothes, shoes and accessories and has a corresponding budget will certainly find what he or she is looking for. If you're staying in Verona during the time of the Saldi (sales), you will have the chance to find a bargain or two for less money.

The Via Mazzini itself was lined with warehouses and barracks until the 19th century. The unfortified ground turned into a veritable mud field during rain showers until the city government decided to secure the street and pave it with marble. The paving was also the reason for the street's rising fortunes barracks gave way to modern stores until the street reached its current appearance. Incidentally, the road was named in 1907 after the Italian politician and philosopher Giuseppe Mazzini (1805-1872), who did much for his country during the Italian Risorgimento and the struggle for freedom.

Biblioteca Capitolare

Oldest library in the world in Verona

The Biblioteca Capitolare is one of the world's oldest libraries and was established in around 517 A.D. as a writing workshop for the cathedral. The massive collection of 75,000 books, manuscripts, codices, parchments and pieces of music is unique. Among the library's valuable pieces are three very important documents: the "Gospel Purpureum" from the 5th Century, an issue of the "Divine Comedy" by Dante and the "De civitate Dei" by St. Augustine. Even the manuscripts of the Roman philosopher Cicero can be found in the collection of the Biblioteca Capitolare.

The chapter library in Verona is unfortunately not open to the public and can only be viewed by making an appointment in advance. Interested visitors should make an appointment and visit this stunning collection

Galleria d'arte moderna

Municipal gallery of modern art

The Galleria d'arte moderna (gallery of modern art) opened its doors to the public in 1982. Its permanent exhibition includes historical and contemporary works by artists from the last two centuries. Among them are artists such as Giulio Paolini, Felice Casorati, Vanessa Beecroft, Guido Trentini and Francesco Hayez.

The foundation of the building, the Palazzo Forti, is from the 13th century. In the 15th century it was rebuilt into a luxurious residential palace with many gardens and courtyards by the Emilei family. The Austrian General Radetzky had his general command in the Palazzo during the Austrian occupation of Verona, which explains the building's current appearance.

Juliet's tomb

Tomba di Giulietta and Museo degli Affreschi
Juliet's tomb and frescoes museum

Juliet's tomb is located in the vaults of the Abbey of San Francesco. According to William Shakespeare's play Romeo and Juliet were buried here. Soon after Shakespeare wrote his love story, a real sarcophagus for the lovers was placed in the courtyard of the monastery. The lid of the sarcophagus and the remains inside were taken to a secret location by the Venetian government because they didn't want the two suicides to have too much public attention. Nevertheless, worshipers of the literary lovers still came to the monastery to praise their idols. Even celebrities, like Marie-Louise of Austria, Napoleon's wife, came here. After the visit she had some jewellery made from fragments of the empty sarcophagus.

For a Hollywood film in 1937 the sarcophagus was taken into the convent vaults for filming the death scene, where it can still be admired today.

For particular Romeo and Juliet fans it is even possible to get married in the vault of the tomb.

Fresco museum

Under Juliet's tomb, the monastery houses the Museo degli Affreschi, the frescoes museum, which opened in 1975. It contains numerous frescoes from the palaces of Verona from the 16th to the 18th century. In the courtyard and basement there are sculptures and amphorae from Roman times.

Giardini Giusti

Beautiful Renaissance garden in Verona

The Giradini Giusti is one of the most beautiful gardens in Italy. The Giusti family built the Palazzo Giusti with its beautiful surrounding gardens in the 16th century. In the 19th century the garden was transformed into an English garden, which gave it its current appearance. The beautiful Renaissance garden is dominated by an impressive, ancient cypress tree avenue, which even impressed the poet Goethe. On several terraces marble sculptures, columns cypresses and clipped hedges can be found. At the highest point of the garden is an oversized mask sculpture the "Maskeron". From here you have a wonderful view over the palace and the city.

Museo Lapidario Maffeiano

Archaeological museum of Verona

The Museo Lapidario Maffeiano was established by Francesco Scipione Maffei (1675 1755) between 1718 and 1727. Maffei was a passionate collector of archaeological pieces and had the declared goal of bringing the ancient and classical era to the common people. Many of the treasures were plundered by Napoleon's troops in the 19th century and were taken to Paris.

Although the majority of Maffeis collection is now in Verona once more, a few valuable pieces remained in the Louvre in Paris.

In the courtyard and the portico of the museum there are 230 inscriptions, reliefs, sarcophagi and several sculptures, which Maffei collected and displayed. In the impressive lobby of the Academua Filarmonica you will find sculptures and inscriptions by the Romans and the Etruscans which have been accurately dated. The Lapidary itself has the character of a living room.

Especially worth seeing on the first floor is Italy's largest collection of Greek grave inscriptions (5th century BC to 4th century AD) with detailed descriptions of the daily life of the ancient Greeks. On the second floor, Etruscan urns, finds from the early Venetian time and a Roman sarcophagus of a young man can be found.

Museo Miniscalchi-Erizzo

Museum and family home of the nobility of Verona

You can get a good impression of the palace life of Veronese noblemen at the Palazzo Miniscalchi-Erizzo. The complex, which is still owned by the family foundation, includes a museum and a small part of the palace is also open to the public. When walking through the palace you will get a good impression of the pomp and splendour which the resident noble Miniscalchi-Erizzo family enjoyed. The family's ancestors came from Venice and Bergamo. The Miniscalchi were rich merchants in Bergamo and Francesco Erizzo was the Doge of Venice when the two families allied and settled in Verona.

The building itself has elements from different eras. The façade of the portal along with the superb double-arched windows is late Gothic in style; the rear building is Classical in style. The Museo Miniscalchi-Erizzo features a temporary and a permanent exhibition on two floors. The permanent exhibition contains some impressive bronze statues and pieces from Venetian, Etruscan and Roman times. A small amber altar with a German inscription in the little chapel is one of the highlights of the collection.

Palazzo Maffei

Eye-catching palace at the Piazza delle Erbe

The Palazzo Maffei is located to the northwest of the Piazza delle Erbe. The baroque palace was built in 1668 by Rolando Maffei. As was usual for the time, special emphasis was placed on the effect of the façade many ornaments and sculptures decorate the exterior of the building. From the balustrade the Greek gods Zeus,

Aphrodite, Apollo, Athena, Hermes and Hercules look down on the market life of the square.

On the ground floor of the Palazzo Maffei there is a restaurant facing the market. But you can still enter the courtyard and take a look at the imposing columns inside.

Chiesa San Tomaso

Tomb of Sanmicheli

The inconspicuous Chiesa San Tomaso church is located right next to the Ponte Nuovo del Popolo. The church was built in the 15th century on the foundations of two previous churches and was inaugurated in 1504. The choir wall in the interior was designed by the famous architect Sanmicheli, who is also buried in the Chiesa San Tomaso. The grave of Sanmicheli is in front of the second altar on the right-hand side.

In 1769 the 13-year-old Wolfgang Amadeus Mozart gave an organ recital in the church. He left behind his initials "WSM" (Wolfgang Salisburgensis Mozart) in the wooden pews of the organ. Unfortunately, the organ is not open to the public, which means that the initials can't be viewed. The church itself is still used very extensively, and attempts have been made to make the church services less boring for the children in front of Sanmicheli's grave there is a small sitting area with pens and paper for drawing and painting.

Via Cappello and Porta Leoni

Commercial street in ancient Verona

When on the Via Cappello, most tourists only make it as far as the Casa di Giulietta (Juliet's house), but the Via Cappello with its many shops and restaurants is a popular shopping street for the locals. The Via Cappello was once the main road when you were coming from Bologna and entered the city through the Porta Leoni. The Via Cappello divides at the remains of the old city gate and you can visit the excavations of the Porta Leoni in the middle.

The former name of the Porta Leoni was Porta San Fermo or Arco di Valerio. Its current name owes its origins to the discovery of two statues of a lion that were found during the excavations around the gate.

Ancient Verona

The Porta leoni was built in the 1st century B.C. together with the first city walls, which were subsequently upgraded on several occasions. The Via Cappello formed the cardo maximus of the Roman city and, together with the Corso Porta Borsari and the Corso Sant'Anastasia, divided the city into 4 equal squares. Parts of the defensive wall around the Porta Leoni still remain and are visible in the buildings around they are considered to be the most important surviving monuments of the ancient city of Verona.

Porta Borsari

From the town gate on the Corso Cavour to Castevecchio

The Porta Borsari was built in the 1st century B.C. and marks the southwestern entrance to the ancient Verona. Originally the town gate was called "Porta Iovia" due to its proximity to the temple of Jupiter. The gate received its name in the middle ages when customs officials (=bursarii) were stationed here who taxed the goods. Similar to the Porta Leoni, the Porta Borsari was designed as a small fortress with guard towers, which enclosed a courtyard. Today you can only see the remains of towers facing away from the city.

If you move from the Porta Borsari south on the Corso Cavour, you walk on a 2,000-year-old road. In Roman times the road connected Genoa, Verona and Trieste. The numerous palaces along the road to the Castelvecchio are of particular interest. The Palazzo Bevilacqua and the Palazzo Canossa were both built by Sanmicheli in 1530. In addition to many architectural styles and interesting little details, the high-water marks of the Adige river, which flooded Verona several times in its history, can be seen on many buildings.

Chiesa di San Giorgio in Braida

A former Benedictine monastery along the Adige river

The Chiesa di San Giorgio in Braida is built on the foundations of a Benedictine monastery from the turn of the second millennium. Apart from the beautiful Romanesque bell tower dating from the 12th century, nothing remains of the former monastery today. In the 15th century it fell into the hands of the canons of San Giorgio of Venice who rebuilt it. The beautiful white marble façade still bears the traces of French rifle fire from 1791 when Napoleon took the city of Verona.

In addition to its façade of columns, the beautiful dome, built by Sanmicheli in 1540, is also noteworthy. The rest of the church is made of brick. Inside the beautiful nave you can admire Tintoretto's first masterpiece, "The Baptism of Christ", directly above the entrance. Two other masterpieces by Paolo Veronese can be found around the high altar under the dome: "The

Miracle of St. Barnaby" and the "Martyrdom of St. George."

Chiesa San Lorenzo

A hidden church along the Corso Cavour

You can't see the church of San Lorenzo from the Corso Cavour. You can reach the church via an inconspicuous Gothic archway decorated with statues from the Via Cavour. The church dates from the 12th century and was built using different coloured materials like many other churches in Verona. In the foundations of the left-hand tower you can see very clearly that stones from the Roman arena were used for the construction of the church a white marble stone with a decorative band bears witness to its origins from the Roman venue.

Inside the Chiesa San Lorenzo the apses in the main nave and the transept are worth seeing.

The altarpiece at the main altar was created by Domenico Brusarzio in 1562; the altarpiece of the Renaissance wooden altar in the right apse was created by Girolamo Benaglio.

Palazzo Barbieri Palazzo Municipale

The town hall of Verona

The Palazzo Barbieri is a classical building on the Piazza Brà. It is named after its architect Giuseppe Barbieri, who was in charge of its construction from 1836 to 1848. Originally the building was planed as a *Gran Guardia Nuova* by the Austrian occupiers and built by Barbieri. With its colossal columns and the massive pediment portico, the palace towers majestically over the Piazza Brà.

The Habsburgs used the Palazzo Barbieri as a base for the Austrian troops and coordinated the defence of Verona from here. After Italian unification the building lost its original function and became the seat of the city government. During the Second World War the palace was heavily damaged by airstrikes but was reconstructed very quickly after the war and again used as city hall from 1950 to the present day.

Palazzo della Gran Guardia

The house of the city guard

The Palazzo della Gran Guardia (palace of the grand guard) is located right next to the Portoni della Brà, the old city gate. The palace served as the headquarters and registered office of the city guard and was built in 1610.

The loggia and the parade ground on the ground floor of the palace were designed by Domenico Curtoni. The staircase and upper floor were not completed until 1850. You can see the style of the master builder of Curtoni, Sanmicheli, especially when looking at the twin pillars on the upper floor they imitate Sanmicheli's Porta Palio.

Today, the former city guard is used as a conference centre and as a gallery.

Arsenale Austriaco

Garrison city of the Austrians

From the Ponte Scaligero you can reach the Arsenale Austriaco also known as Arsenal Franz Joseph I via the Piazza Arsenale. The arsenal was built between 1854 and 1861 by Lieutenant Colonel Conrad Petrasch for the Habsburgs and housed Field Marshal Radetzky's troops. Squares, farms, roads, warehouses, barracks, stables, officers' buildings and shops are to be found on 7 hectares almost like in a small isolated town.

After Italian unification the arsenal was left to decay that's the reason why it looks a little bit run down and sad today. But there are plans to restore the Arsenale Austriaco. Parts of the garrison city are to be declared a museum and the arena's foundation is planning to build a cultural centre within the walls of the old arsenal.

Romeo's house

Family seat of the Montecchi

In contrast to Juliet's house, Romeo's house is just a name for the tourists. Its real name is Casa di Cagnolo Nogarola detto Romeo. The house itself is privately owned and lived in, and is unfortunately not open for visitors. However, the beautiful Gothic façade from the 14th century fits well with the famous love story of William Shakespeare, and so countless tourists can be found in front of the house every day, admiring Romeo's house and taking pictures.

It has been proven, however, that the powerful noble family Montecchi formerly resided in this neighbourhood of Verona, and so this inconspicuous place has managed to preserve a little of its fascination concerning the famous love story of Romeo and Juliet.

Verona Surroundings

Destinations in the province of Verona

Not many provinces can offer their visitors as much as Verona. The list of activities and interesting places is long. From Lake Garda and its beach resorts to the hiking area of Mount Baldo and the Bardolino, Valpolicella and Soave vineyards. There are more than enough daytrip destinations if you are staying in Verona, and you should make sure not miss many of these attractions. On ZAINOO you will find a lot of information and numerous tips for travel destinations in the region.

Custoza

Theatre of war around Verona

The small town of Custoza gained notoriety as the setting for two big battles. In 1848 the Austrians under Field Marshall Radetzky defeated the rebellious Italians. In 1866 the Italians lost a second time in the same place against the Austrians this time under the leadership of Archduke Albrecht. In memory of the many casualties of these battles a vast charnel house (ossario) was erected in Custoza. It has the form of an obelisk and is placed on a hill visible for all from far away. From the top of the obelisk you have a wonderful view over the surrounding countryside. In the basement, thousands of bones form a huge pile a silent witness to the cruel slaughter.

Soave

Origin of an excellent white wine

The beautiful wine village of Soave is surrounded by kilometres of vineyards. Soave has a very special medieval flair which you won't find in many other medieval cities. The centre is completely surrounded by a well-preserved city wall with many towers an impressive Scaliger castle is enthroned on a hill above the city. Through small narrow streets you reach the Palazzo di Giustizia, which has a beautiful column loggia. From here you can climb up to the Scaliger castle, which is not as well preserved as the city walls. In the surviving part of the castle is a museum with historical armour and furniture. From the battlements of the defensive wall you have a beautiful view over the city and the surrounding vineyards.

Soave an excellent white wine

The world-famous "Soave" (= soft) white wine matures in the surrounding vineyards. Soave has long been one of the most popular white wines in Italy. According to a legend, its name owes its origin to the famous poet Dante Alighieri. Despite its fame, the wine has fallen into disrepute in recent years. High demand induced many growers to produce greater, but significantly worse in terms of quality, quantities of wine. More and more growers are returning to the traditional wine growing process, which is a bit more expensive but results in more tasty wines. If you want to taste a really good wine, you will find one in Soave for sure.

Valpolicella

Famous wine region north of Verona

The Valpolicella, the valley of the many cellars, extends just north of Verona and offers a nice contrast to the densely populated urban area. Shortly after the city limits, the road goes up in several hairpin bends and winding roads into the hills of the Valpolicella where countless vines and fruit trees dominate the landscape. Many magnificent mansions and villas rise up among the vineyards and give the region an additional charm. Many of these magnificent villas are open to visitors where you will have the chance to taste one or two drops of excellent wine. Even Dante Alighieri's descendants have settled in the Valpolicella. On the large estate of the Alighieris, the Villa Serego Alighieri, you can taste some wines and also spend the night.

The most famous wines of Valpolicella are the "Valpolicella" itself, the "Recioto" and the

"Amarone". The name "Valpolicella" means valley of many cellars and owes its origins, of course, to the many wine cellars of the estates that are scattered throughout the valley.

Palladian Villa in the Valpolicella
Although it is an inconspicuously located village, the wine centre of Pedemonte northwest of Verona is an extraordinary sight. The Villa Serego Santa Sofia is the only Palladian villa in the Verona region. Unfortunately, the villa was never completed the impressive two-tier portico with giant Ionic columns is nevertheless a fascinating sight. The villa is now restored and is part of the Santa Sofia winery. Interested parties should register with the host and, if you are lucky, you can take a closer look at the beautiful villa.

Giardino di Pojega in Negrar
Also northwest of Verona is the small wine-growing village of Negrar. It houses one of the

biggest attractions of the Valpolicella the Giardino di Pojega. The beautiful garden belonging to the villa Rizzardi by Luigi Trezza was built half in English, half in Italy style and is well worth visiting. The garden is can be viewed on Thursday and Saturday afternoon visitors can taste and purchase the homemade wines.

Lombard-Romanesque church

Getting to the small village of San Giorgio di Valpolicella located on a hill in the west of the Valpolicella is not easy. From the church you have a wonderful view over the Valpolicella and Lake Garda. The Lombard-Romanesque church of San Giorgio from the 13th century is worth a visit. Inside the church there are remains of old frescoes, an octagonal baptistery and a Lombard column altar from the 8th century. The church's picturesque cloister is a fitting conclusion to the tour.

Tregnago

Small vinicultural village with Scaliger castle

The area around Tregnago was already populated during the times of Roman colonialization and remained an important strategic place for the rulers of Verona up into the 15th century. Among the fascinating sights in the village centre are Chiesa della Disciplina known for its art treasures including beautiful 14th century frescoes by Giolfino and a relief made from white marble and Villa Carlo Cipolla. The latter was built in the 16th century as the domicile of the noble Cipolla family. In recent years the villa became property of the winemaker Pieropan, who turned it into a site for events.

Scaliger castle

The medieval Scaliger castle, which can be reached from village centre after a 15-minute walk, rises high above the place. The castle lost a lot of its importance starting in the 15th century, but is being used again nowadays for medieval events and festivities. The annual Medievalia festival, which celebrates life in the Middle Ages with medieval games and festivities, takes place here in September.

Industry in Tregnago

After World War I an industrial centre developed in Tregnago as in many other places, too. The foundation of the cement plant Italcementi in 1922 played a major role in the region's boom preventing the population's emigration. In the 1960s the construction crisis lead to the closing of the plant. Today the old plant's ruins are renovated gradually and integrated into new projects. A new school was built here recently the exquisite ice cream parlour "La Fabbrica" amidst the historical ruins is a grand culinary tip.

The village today mainly lives on its numerous vines and winemakers.

Bolca

Fossil site

Inconspicuously situated but of historical significance is the small village of Bolca. It gained world fame on account of the many fossils that can be found in the surrounding limestone mountains. Several metres thick, the limestone layers hide huge quantities of fossil some of them are preserved so well that scientists could determine organs and skin colour of the fish and marine creatures that lived 50 million years ago!

You can see many of the fascinating exhibits in the Museo dei fossils (fossils museum) in the city. A special aquarium featuring the fossils' descendants provides visitors with interesting insights. Those who are interested can also go down to the fossil site on a special trail and walk along the million-year-old stone tombs. The museum is closed on Mondays.

Villafranca di Verona

Southern bastion of the Scaliger

Villafranca di Verona is located just south of Verona Airport and was one of the main southern bastions of the Scala family. With its still mighty appearance, the Scaliger castle in the city entre was part of a major line of defence against the south from Sirmione on Lake Garda via Villa Franca to Sanguinetto. 8 large square towers protect the city walls from the outside. The main tower (Mastio) and a resistance museum (Museo del Risorgimento) can be visited on the weekends.

Also worth seeing is the Museo Nicolis, which includes a large exhibition on the development of traffic and transport systems. The museum is especially famous for its unique classic car, bicycle and motorcycle collection.

Illasi

Scaliger castle and wine-growing village east of Verona

The wine-growing village of Illasi impresses with two main sights. Two beautiful villas from the 17th centruy and a powerful Scala family castle on the hill above the town. The two villas from the 17th century were built by the Veronese noble family of Pompei and have beautiful gardens and rich frescoes. The villa Sagramoso Perez-Pompei and the Villa Carlotti Perez-Pompei are located in the north of the town and are unfortunately closed for visitors. The Scaliger castle can be reached by a winding road that branches off at the church in the village on the left-hand side. At the end of the road a 20-minute walk leads to the castle. The castle is also closed for visitors but the magnificent view over the Veneto and the beautiful backdrop of the castle make this trip worthwhile.

Scaliger castle in Tregnago

Only 5 kilometres north of Illasi is the small village of Tregnago. In a 15-minute walk you can reach an impressive Scaliger castle on the hill above the village. At both castles Illasi and Tregnago Roman watchtowers have been preserved. The same is true of the Scaliger castle in Soave. This suggests a sophisticated Roman security system. Each tower can be seen from the next. In case of emergency the towers could warn the entire region very quickly with balefires.

Monte Lessini

Across the Lessin mountains

The Lessin mountains extend north from Verona from the Valpolicella region to the Alps and they already have a pretty alpine character. The mountains rise up around five valleys up to 1,700 metres and have been used as quarries by their inhabitants since ancient times. The famous red marble, which can be admired in many places in Verona, comes from the Lessin mountains. Besides the marble, the limestone is mined in the mountains and used for roofs, road courses and squares in the surrounding cities. The Lessin mountains offer visitors a beautiful scenic landscape. From massive natural monuments to densely wooded mountains, picturesque valleys and spectacular fossils and prehistoric relics there's a lot to see in the Lessin mountains.

Parco Naturale delle Cascate and the Museo Paleontologico e Preistorico

In the Parco Naturale delle Cascate near the village of Molina is a junction of three valleys, where a number of impressive waterfalls plunge into the depths. The beautiful landscape of the park can be explored on various marked trails. The small village of Sant'Anna d'Alfaedo is located to the north of Molina. It is the location of the Museo e Paleontologico Preistorico (Paleontology and Prehistoric Museum), which, among many other spectacular fossils, exhibits a 7-metre-long fossilised shark from the Tethys Sea as its main attraction.

Ponte di Veja natural monument

You will find a natural attraction of a very special kind to the south of Sant'Anna d'Alfaedo. A 50-metre-long and 30-metre-high giant rock arch, the Ponte di Veja. The gigantic arch spans the river and is a very impressive natural wonder which you must see if you are in the region. At the same time the Ponte di Veja formas the entrance to a cave where prehistoric findings were made. Because of its prehistoric importance the cave is not open to visitors. Back at the car park you can taste some traditional Venetian food in the local trattoria.

In the eastern foothills of the Lessin mountains, the small village of Camposilvano offers various attractions. Besides the Museo Geo-Paleontologico with its fossils and prehistoric discoveries, the Valle delle Sfingi is a visit worth. The beautiful valley north of the village fascinates its visitors with its unique mushroom-shaped karst monoliths which are scattered throughout the valley.

Isola della Scala

Rice-growing region in the south of Veneto

The Isola della Scala is often called "Città del Riso" (city of rice) because it is surrounded by large rice fields. It has been a centre of rice production in Veneto since the 17th century. The city itself is home to 10,500 inhabitants and contains little worth seeing. At the staircase to the church you can see a historic water wheel from the rice plant of the Ferron family. At the end of the town you will find the Church Santuario della Madonna della Bastia with some preserved frescoes in the interior. Near the church you can have a look at the Torre Skaliger from the 12thcentury, which are ringed by a moat.

Fiera del Riso rice festival

Once a year between September and October, the Fiera del Riso takes place in Isola della Scala. This event starts immediately after the rice harvest in autumn and many culinary contests and historical exhibitions inspire visitors. The rice festival is, of course, not only an event for informing and watching but also for tasting hundreds of thousands of different risotto recipes are served during the event..

History of rice cultivation in Isola della Scala

Rice has been grown around the Isola della Scala since the 17th century. Although the major rice growing areas in Italy are located in the Po Valley, the Isola della Scala has managed to develop into an impressive rice cultivation area. Many major rice producers like Ferron, Melotti, Riccò, del Vò and Rancan have their rice mills and numerous shops and restaurants here. The Ferron family in particular, stands for successful rice cultivation tradition in the region. The family's old rice mill, the Antica Riseria Ferron, is north of Isola della Scala on the SS12 and is still open for visits.

Family Trip with Kids

Family trip to Verona with children. Ideas on where to go with your child

The town of Verona is famous for its historical monuments and museums. However, not only lovers of excursions will like to have a vacation here, but also tourists with children. In the city, there are excellent conditions for active recreation. In addition to popular bicycle tours, the entertainment center King Rock arrampicata is in demand among tourists with children. It is a huge climbing wall with many walls of different levels of complexity. Both visitors with children and professional climbers will be able to be perfectly entertained here. Many choose the center for family holidays. For visitors, interesting games are organized here and they are offered to pass various obstacle courses.

Guests with older children will have the opportunity to visit the paragliding center located in Verona –Yeti Extreme Tandem Paragliding Flights. Paragliding flights are conducted in the picturesque countryside, and are accessible to everyone, even children. They are offered the opportunity to fly over the spacious green meadows together with an instructor who manages the paraglider. The whole family is guaranteed mass impressions from such extreme entertainment. Those who are not new to the sport are offered to rent all necessary equipment in the center.

With teenagers, you can go on a fascinating walk through the picturesque Parco delle Cascate di Molina Park. This natural reserve is very large and beautiful. Its main attraction is waterfalls. The reserve is simply designed for walking. Close to all waterfalls and other famous landmarks are equipped comfortable observation platforms, and above some waterfalls you can even ride on a swing. The reserve is situated in a picturesque mountainous area and several historical buildings have been preserved on its territory. One of the most fascinating stages of the excursion promises to be a walk through the local grottoes. Vacationers with children should take into account that in the caves, it is pretty cool even in summer, so it is worth taking warm clothes along.

Nature lovers who do not expect to go on such long walks during the holidays should take a peek into the Palazzo Giardino Giusti garden. This garden is incredibly beautiful. In the warm season, it is always decorated with a lot of interesting landscape compositions. Children will definitely like to walk among the spreading trees and active labyrinths. In a small pond in the park, they will be able to watch turtles. In the vast garden, there are also quite concealed corners ideal for a relaxing holiday. From the viewing platforms, one can see an attractive view of the historic district of Verona. The garden is very well maintained, and there are equipped picnic areas on its territory.

Among the numerous museums in Verona, it is worth noting the Museo Civico di Storia Naturale. This natural history museum will be especially interesting to visit with children. The museum is located in a beautiful historic building, and features a rich collection of exhibits dedicated to the diversity of wildlife. Here, there are realistic models of lizards and dinosaurs, paintings and photographs depicting rare insects, and skeletons of rare animals, including prehistoric ones. The collection of ancient fossils on which one can make out the skeletons of fishes that inhabited the sea in prehistoric times, as well as shells of mollusks, is of particular interest. In this museum, special excursions are carried out for children, and it will be interesting for adults to get acquainted with its collection. In Verona, absolutely everyone will be able to choose the entertainment of their taste, including fans of extreme sports, and fans of excursions.

Cuisine and Restaurant

Cuisine of Verona for gourmets. Places for dinner - best restaurants

The local cuisine is quite diversified. Chefs of Verona are the authors of many well-known dishes that are popular among gourmets around the world. Each restaurant of national cuisine will surely offer its guests to try «gnocchi» potato dumplings, which are usually served with various sauces. Among the most popular first course dishes you will find «Risotto al tastasal» - a tender risotto, which is cooked from pork mince.

It's simply impossible to imagine a meal without the famous «polenta» corn porridge, which is now offered to guests of all Italian restaurants. Local chefs cook polenta in accordance with classic recipes with the addition of various sauces. Fans of gourmet dishes are welcome to order porridge with wild game, and vegetarian food devotees will surely like polenta with cheese. Fans of "hotter" food will fall in love with «Bollito con la pearà» meat. Slices of boiled meat seasoned with spices are served with a special hot sauce, which is used for cooking meat broth, cheese and bread.

Among classic meat dishes we should definitely mention "Brasato di manzo all'Amarone" beef braised in wine, which, according to connoisseurs of Italian cuisine, has simply incomparable taste. Beef is also used to cook a not less attractive dish called «peperate» - meat is stewed with spices and fragrant cheese. Simply no Italian restaurant is possible to imagine without rich choice of spaghetti and pasta. In Verona «bigoli» is considered the most popular type of pasta. Connoisseurs of meat delicacies will also like «pastisada de caval» dish, which is prepared according to original recipe and is made of high quality horse meat.

Despite the fact that many meat dishes make up the basis of the menu of every restaurant, gastronomic facilities of Verona will be liked by fans of fish dishes as well. In Lake Garda are found several species of fish, which are baked with vegetables, grilled and stewed with spicy sauces by skilled chefs. If you want to try an authentic Verona dessert, you should definitely try «croccante» almond biscuits, as well as «Sbrisolona» cake. On Christmas Eve numerous vendors from street fairs offer passers-by to try flavored «Pandoro» cakes, and before Easter local bakers made their signature «Colomba» cakes. Rich selection of wines in local restaurants and cafes is worth a separate mentioning. Such sorts as Valpolicella, Bardolino, Amarone, Custoza, Lugana and Recioto di Valpolicella are considered the most popular.

Farcito is a popular restaurant where visitors can try the most popular dishes of the regional cuisine. The restaurant's chefs are true wizards who turn even simple ingredients into true culinary masterpieces. Among the signature dishes, it is important to mention potatoes baked with vegetables, salads with fresh cheese and ham, different variations of pizza and sandwiches. Despite the fact that the majority of dishes are cooked in accordance with quite simple recipes, all food looks attractive and appetizing. Best Italian wine, which is also present in the menu, will only help visitors to enjoy their meal.

The next restaurant in our review, Salumeria Gironda, offers not only the most popular Italian cuisine dishes but also Mediterranean ones. It is a great choice for everyone who likes seafood. Many praise Salumeria Gironda for a range of local meat delicacies and cheese that are delivered from the nearby farms. Even a simple meal with these products together with freshly baked bread and a bottle of Italian wine can easily turn into an unforgettable one.

Archivio is a popular restaurant that specializes in fusion cuisine. The menu is full of interesting snacks and appetizers. Besides that, Archivio always offers signature beverages made of fresh fruit. The small restaurant is an incredibly charming and friendly place, so it is very popular with local youth.

Parma a Tavola specializes in cooking classic Italian cuisine. The restaurant's menu features dozens of pasta types, a fabulous choice of ravioli, and the signature lasagna. Moreover, Parma a Tavola offers interesting organic delicacies, including gorgeous cheese platters, sausage and bacon plates. The latter always comes with delicious olives.

Zio Lele is one of the most popular pizzerias in Verona. It offers dozens of pizza types, including special pizza for vegetarian visitors. Zio Lele is a great choice for a family dinner. Besides pizza, the restaurant sells fresh bread cooked in an authentic oven.

Travelers, who cannot imagine a meal without an attractive and eye-catching dessert in the end, should definitely visit Carducci. Each dish in this café has a mesmerizing design. Carducci offers delicious pastries and light desserts in the Italian style. Besides pastries and desserts, the café offers mouthwatering meat dishes and various salads. Fans of fine Italian cheese will also enjoy their visit to Carducci.

Tradition and Lifestyle

Colors of Verona - traditions, festivals, mentality and lifestyle

Many people think of a touching love story of Romeo and Juliet when they hear the word "Verona". Indeed, the plot of the famous tragedy by Shakespeare took place here. Each year the city hosts the most romantic festival in the world - Verona in Love - which always attracts a large number of travelers. The festival starts February 12 and lasts for three days. As you can guess from the name, the main theme of the festival is triumph of love. During three days streets of Verona are decorated huge posters, lights and balloons in the shape of hearts. You can see words on these huge colorful posters - lovers use them to confess their feelings. The celebration traditionally attracts a large number of couples.

During the festival the streets of the city become the location for wonderful presentations, interesting events and fairs, where visitors can various interesting souvenirs and gifts for their beloved ones. The main celebrations are held near the house of Juliet, as well as on St. Anastasia Square. The biggest fair is located on Dei Signori Square. Stalls here are set in heart shape. You will see many interesting gifts, sweets and decorations in these festive outlets. Rides in beautiful carriages drawn by white horses are another very popular entertainment among vacationers.

Numerous restaurants of the city also prepare special offers for their guests. You will simply not find such a huge amount of romantic dishes at any other holiday - cakes in the shape of hearts, candy and fruit salads decorated in festive style will surely be a great addition to the holiday. Fans of unusual events have an opportunity to visit tasting events and master classes dedicated to cooking dishes from aphrodisiacs, and fans of excursions will be offered to visit the most romantic places of Verona.

It's worth noting that Verona attracts a large number of couples not only during the festival. This is a popular place to conduct solemn wedding ceremonies and honeymoon vacations, celebrating wedding anniversaries and other memorable dates. The unique atmosphere of romance and mystery is always found in Verona. This is a beautiful and charming city with interesting and multifaceted culture.

It's hard to find those who have never heard about the openness of Italians, and in Verona, this openness is very evident. Locals are always ready to help if tourists need an assistance. To attitude to life is relaxed and positive. Another quality of local residents is the break of distance, which happens very quickly, and they have no equal in this. You should be prepared for the fact that during the time from 1:00 PM to 3:00 PM (sometimes even up to 5:00 pm) many facilities, including shops, may be closed - it's Verona siesta. The so-called "familiness" also distinguishes the local residents. And, of course, romanticism - that's what fully characterizes people who live here. After all, how could it be otherwise in the city of love and romance?

Another festival associated with the City of Everlasting Love is Carnevale di Verona that traces its roots from ancient times. It begins in early January and lasts until the end of the third month of winter. In early February, spectators are waiting for Venerdì Gnocolar where they can witness the election of Papà del Gnoco followed by a fashion show. There are parades, theme nights, afterparties during the carnival. The festival is a must for those who want to get closer acquainted with the local culture.

Another event that often comes to mind when mentioning Verona is known as Arena di Verona Festival. Despite the fact that it is believed that the opera is boring, the event will surely convince even the most skeptical critics otherwise. Firstly, it is a grandiose show and entertainment, for which you should definitely attend Arena di Verona. Secondly, the beauty of the arena - that's where you can realize how good the Romans were at erecting majestic buildings, and accordingly, the love of the Italians for grandiose shows. And, of course, the mood of the festival - the audience is immersed in an extraordinary atmosphere where it is impossible to understand where the reality ends. The festival is held between the end of June and the end of August.

There is also the love for hard rock in Verona, as evidenced by holding Rock the Castle beginning in late June and ending in early July. It takes place in Castello Scaligero (located in Villafranca di Verona), which gives the festival some staginess and spectacularity. Among the festival headliners you can rarely see the names you've never heard before; the event is popular among youth, and it's always a great honor for participants to perform at such a grandiose festival - after all, Verona people cannot make up a show program in a different way - their love for all grandiose and majestic can be considered a synonym.

Another remarkable festival is On Stage. More precisely, this is a project that unites large cities and is aimed at attracting interest in traveling and tourism. It is held in early April, and the whole city turns into its stage. During this time, on central city streets, you can hear music, attend master classes, watch theatrical and dance performances, and go on excursions. Thanks to the festival, you can learn a lot of new things about the local culture, traditions, and history, as well as just be very impressed.

Italians are famous for their love for pleasures, and one of these pleasures is food. Well, you should never deny yourself this. And therefore gastronomic festivals held in the country always attract a lot of visitors. They include Vinitaly taking place in the middle of April. The main city streets become the venue for the event, and many local restaurants are happy to join it. Vinitaly's program includes wine tasting, theatrical performances, consultations on interesting questions about selecting and making wines. Without exaggeration, this is the largest festival of its kind in Italy, and therefore no tourist should miss the opportunity to attend it while in the City of Romance.

In early October, you can witness such an event as Verona Food Truck Festival. As you can guess from the name, during this time on the central streets you can see many food trucks, which means that you need to use the excellent opportunity to sample fine cuisines from around the world. The most popular food is pizza, ice cream, burritos, and tacos. The festival is also participated by local restaurants and cafes. All kinds of performances and a music show are prepared for the audience in addition to the gastronomic program.

Culture of Verona

Places to visit - old town, temples, theaters, museums and palaces

Piazza delle Erbe is the most famous square of Verona. Near it you will find several major architectural landmarks of the city. Here you will see the beautiful palace of Maffei, as well as House of the Merchants and Torre del Gardello. The construction of the tower was completed in 1370. The tower is distinguished by original style.

In 1626, during the restoration of the tower, it was enlarged and new details were added to it.

Case Mazzanti is a beautiful architectural monument of the Middle Ages. It was built in the 16th century. Its facade is decorated with artful murals, which depict scenes from various ancient myths. There are also some monuments of Roman times which have survived in Verona. Amphitheatre is considered the most famous among them. According to archaeologists, it was built in the 1st century BC. This is a massive structure, during the construction of which was used rare marble. According to preliminary calculations, the amphitheater could accommodate about 30,000 spectators.

Vacationers should definitely not forget to see the beautiful arch bridge of Ponte Pietra, the building of was also conducted yet in the prehistoric era. The bridge was seriously damaged during the Second World War, but thanks to efforts of skilled architects it was restored. Santa Maria Antica Church remains one of the most interesting religious sites of the city. This is a beautiful building made in the Romanesque style. For a long time it was used as a family chapel for privileged persons. The first church was built yet in the 7th century, but the building was completely destroyed by a strong earthquake. The cathedral, which visitors can see today, was built in the end of 12th century. The magnificent building is made in best traditions of Romanesque style.

There is one more important sightseeing destination near the church old Ponte Scaligero. Near the church are buried the members of the noble della Scala family. Their tombs are decorated with artful and architectural monuments. Fans of the famous Shakespeare's tragedy should definitely visit the house of Juliet. In the 13th century the beautiful mansion belonged to Dal Capello family, which was used as the prototype of the Capulet family. There is also a house of Romeo in Verona a beautiful building of the 14th century made in Gothic style. Despite the fact that these attractions have no real connection with literary heroes, travelers still believe in the beautiful legend and keep visiting these romantic places.

But the sights of this city, immortalized by Shakespeare, do not end there. The Teatro Romano, a spectacular ruin in the center of Verona, where unimaginably beautiful views of the river open up, has become a compulsory route. Here on the top floor, is located the Museo Archeologico, where among the exhibits are findings discovered during excavations. Rising even higher, you can find a cafe where you can sit perfectly while enjoying picturesque views. It would be particularly great if you visit a cafe with your second half many do so. Verona is precisely associated with romance and love.

Palazzo della Ragione is another interesting place judging from its architectural layout. This kind of architecture although not typical of the architecture of the Middle Ages, also attracts attention immediately it is gazed upon. This red and white building was built in the 12th century (though the first buildings on this place were built even earlier), but since then, it has been rebuilt more than once. The most attractive place to visit is the courtyard, the building being famous for its unrivaled gothic staircase. Another palace, the Palazzo Giardino Giusti, astonishes with its romantic view. You should as a matter of necessity, visit it if you are traveling with your better half. The cypress trees growing here are interesting, and the beautiful fountains and sculptures add to the romantic feel as well.

You certainly cannot pass by an elegant and majestic building such as the Arca di Cansignorio without becoming fascinated by it. It is one of the most beautiful places in the city. Besides, it is one of the symbols of the city, immortalized by Shakespeare. Its arch was built in the 13th-14th centuries in the Gothic style. It is in fact, a tomb, where they buried the representatives of the Scaliger dynasty who ruled Verona during those times. However the best views of the capital of romance can be seen, if you climb up the tower Torre dei Lamberti. The time of its construction dates back to the 12th century, but despite this, the tower is still the tallest building in the city. Thus, it would not be strange if you become surprised by the unprecedented craftsmanship of the builders and engineers of that time.

Talking about the interesting museums in the city, first of all, it is worth noting the Museo di Castelvecchio. Besides the fact that there are beautiful entertaining exhibits here (frescoes, sculptures, paintings of the 14th-16th centuries), the building is also attractive from an architectural point of view. Especially striking are the views from the interior on the Skaliger's Bridge, which is beautifully illuminated in the evening. The Il Museo Del Giocattolo will appeal to even the youngest visitors, as hundreds of toys are displayed there. The Museo Canonicale is also architecturally interesting. It is located in the Complesso della Cattedrale-Duomo courtyard. Beautiful exhibits are also represented here, among them, church utensils, and works of sacred art.

Attraction and Nightlife

City break in Verona. Active leisure ideas for Verona - attractions, recreation and nightlife

Without a doubt, shopping remains one of main entertainments of travelers. Luxury boutiques and modern shopping centers, souvenir shops and interesting markets welcome visitors simply every day. A large part of luxury shops and boutiques is located on Corso Santa Anastasia Street. This is a great place to purchase fashionable apparel from top designers of Italy. Via Mazzini is an ideal place for walks. The street is home to numerous attractive shops and several interesting restaurants, as well as architectural and historical places of interest.

Corso Porta Borsari Street is the location of wonderful clothing stores. Here you will find shopping pavilions that sell classic casual clothing and holiday apparel, and, of course, numerous pretty accessories. Tourists, who prefer to purchase antiques as souvenirs, are recommended to visit the market located on San-Zeno Square. Among the goods sold here you will find beautiful paintings and antique statues, utensils made of precious metals, as well as a lot of other interesting crafts and antiques.

Most popular souvenir shops are located close to Juliet's house. It should be noted that miniature figurines depicting Shakespeare's characters remain the leaders in turns of popularity among souvenirs. Verona Centro Commerciale Le Corti Venete and Grand'Affi Shopping Center are the most popular large-scale shopping centers. The latter is located near Lake Garda and offers customers a wide selection of products, starting from clothes and shoes by local manufacturers to exotic plants and crafts. Local wine is a no less popular souvenir, which can be purchased ir of numerous specialty shops.

People, who want to escape from bustle of the city and spend a day outdoors, are recommended to visit the beautiful garden of Giusti (Palazzo e Giardino Giusti). There is an ancient palace in the territory of the garden. The palace is surrounded by cypresses and huge flower beds on all sides. During a walk through the shady alleys of the garden, travellers will see beautiful statues and fountains depicting ancient heroes. Some of the figures are made of rare red marble.

The City Of Love And Romance is a great place to spend a great time actively. Thus, for those wishing to go climbing, there is King Rock arrampicata, which, among other things, will be of great interest to small children. Well, tourists who want to get a stronger dose of an extreme hormone contact Volo Biposto Parapendio or Yeti Extreme Tandem Paragliding Flights providing skydiving opportunities. And since this kind of leisure leaves only pleasant impressions, you should not miss your chance. Feel the adrenaline rush by visiting A.S.D. Verona Paintball, and it is not necessary to be a paintball enthusiast for this.

When it comes to water types of entertainment, rafting is particularly popular here, and in order to try it, please pay attention to Verona Rafting and Adige Rafting. Golf players go to Easy Golf Verona to enjoy their favorite noble sport, and Minigolf di Torricelle is suitable for playing its mini version. Those who prefer billiards to all other games will appreciate Sala Verona and what they can get by visiting the facility. And these are only bright emotions and pleasant impressions. The same impressions can be found at Bowling Verona. For those who want to swim, it is worthwhile to visit Piscina Villafranca or Piscine Santini where this desire can be fully satisfied.

Look for rentals to explore multiple city attractions, and the best option in this case will be a bicycle ideally suited for the Verona streets. Companies you need are Veronality, Verona Run Bike, Green Bike Verona, Verona Bike, Bicicaffe, In Tandem. You can also rent a scooter, for this, you should contact Due Ruote Verona. Well, a very interesting pastime option would be a small truck tour from Risciò Solidale. As well as escape quests where you can demonstrate your wit and ingenuity. The best facilities of this kind are Intrappola, Play the City, Effugio, Cronos, and AcEscape.

If there is a desire to watch the latest premieres, head to the best cinema in the City of Everlasting Love, namely to Cinema Pindemonte. There are a lot of cultural institutions for enjoying all kinds of performances in Verona. You shouldn't ignore such places as Arena di Verona, Teatro Romano, Villa InCanto Opera Lirica, and Teatro Stabile di Verona. It is worth noting that this is a kind of symbol of Verona, and therefore missing the opportunity to attend grandiose and colorful theatrical productions is not acceptable.

Two statues in the city are worthy of separate mention. First of all, we are talking about the monument to Juliet. It is believed that if you touch Juliet's heart (the girl's right breast) and think about your soulmate, the dream will come true and love will never die. By the way, marriage ceremonies are often held on Juliet's balcony, and this is not surprising, because it's hard to imagine a more romantic place. Another interesting monument is the sculpture of Dante Alighieri, next to which you can often see cooing lovers or friends - this is a very popular meeting place. Nearby is Torre dei Lamberti ideal for admiring panoramic views of the unusually beautiful city. Especially if you're visiting the tower in the evening, during sunset.

The city has a lot of truly unique museums. Of course, first of all, it is worth noting the "calling card" of the city - Casa di Giulietta, next to which stands the above-mentioned monument to the protagonist of the Shakespeare's tragedy. Archeology buffs go to Museo Archeologico and Museo Archeologico al Teatro Romano, and those who wish to "touch the history" - to Museo di Castelvecchio. Museo Civico di Storia Naturale will impress lovers of natural sciences and children, while art connoisseurs prefer Arena

Museo Opera, Galleria d'Arte Moderna Palazzo Forti, Museo degli Affreschi. With small citizens, it will be very interesting to visit Museo della Radio and Museo Conte delle Arti Grafiche.

Verona nightlife also has something to offer. Thus, jazz lovers meet at Jazz and More Bar, those who want to feel the atmosphere of a pub go to Celtic Pub Verona, and Amadeus bar is for those who are primarily interested in an original interior. Spend a quiet and relaxing time sitting in Art Cafe Verona, and have fun in TIFFANY bar where studying alcoholic beverages presented on the menu may take hours. For a sweet tooth, it would be nice to visit Art & Chocolate Gallery Cafe, and Dorian Gray will surely please all those wishing to go crazy dancing until dawn.

Tips for Tourist

Preparing your trip to Verona: advices & hints - things to do and to obey

1. Tourists, who expect to devote much time to walks and excursions around the city, are recommended to visit Verona during the period from early May to early October. At this time of year the weather is most favorable, so long rains will not spoil your recreation program.

2. There is a tourist office next to Porta Nuova railway station. You can obtain a free map of the city there. The map is very useful as it shows all public transport routes and throws the light upon the upcoming cultural events.

3. Buses remain the main form of public transport. Tickets must be purchased in advance. They are sold in all newspaper and tobacco kiosks. As a rule, tickets vary in price and are valid for a certain period of time.

4. Lake Garda can be reached by special blue buses that start their route from the square near the station. If you expect to travel a lot around the city and use public transport for that purpose, it is better to purchase a special ticket named Verona Card. This pass provides its holder with a discount not only for public transport, but also for various museums and theaters.

5. Getting around the city by car can be quite problematic. During rush hours there are heavy traffic jams on all main streets of the city. The historic center of the city is a pedestrian area. Motorists are allowed to drive there in certain hours only.

6. You can easily obtain a free copy of «Verona Guida alla shopping» booklet at the tourist office. The booklet provides a detailed description of all

shops and shopping centers of the city, including their specificity and working hours.

7. Travellers who want to save money on restaurants, should pay attention to local residents. If there are many visitors in a restaurant, then this place is distinguished bot only by a great menu but also by reasonable prices.

8. The most beneficial way to make phone calls to other cities and countries is to use special telephone tubes that are located close to all major shopping malls, banks and transport stops. You can pay for your calls with coins or by using a special plastic card. You can also purchase special phone cards. They are usually sold in all newspaper and tobacco kiosks.

9. Travellers, who plan to use mobile phones during their vacation, should not forget that roaming in Verona is quite expensive.

10. Despite the fact that the Verona is a fairly safe city, travelers should follow basic security precautions. All valuable items are better to be kept in a safe at your hotel. Do not leave your belongings in public places and do not leave bags and outerwear unattended

Accommodation

Stylish Design-Hotels

Some hotels in Verona are characterized by an inimitable design, including upscale Lady Capulet Apartments. Its customers have only four available rooms equipped in one of the invaluable historic buildings. Apartments feature elegant antique furniture, the upholstery of which is made of velvet fabric of purple and scarlet colors. All rooms are covered with lovely wallpapers in the style of the past, while high ceilings and beams preserved inside make the interior truly special.

Hotel Giberti

From Verona center - 0.9 km

A very beautiful modern building with a glazed facade of undulating shape is occupied by Hotel Giberti. The basis of its refined and elegant interior is a chic finish of rare marble and wood, and the abundance of fresh flowers gives the atmosphere a romantic mood. On the hotel's ground floor, there is a very beautiful seating area with dazzling-white soft furniture decorated with exquisite carpets in the spirit of the past. Despite the fact that the hotel's interior includes a lot of fine and complex elements, it doesn't seem overloaded at all.

Opera Relais De Charme

From Verona center - 0.2 km

There is a hotel suitable for opera fans in Verona - they are served by Opera Relais De Charme. Its charming rooms and apartments are decorated in a unique style, their design is dedicated to world-famous operas. All the rooms are decorated with interesting thematic paintings that look like posters, as well as with designer furniture of original shapes and different colors. Chic vintage mirrors in carved gilded frames and an abundance of luxurious fabrics help to emphasize the aristocratic design.

Il Vicolo Residence

From Verona center - 1 km

Behind the walls of a strict 17th-century historic building, there is an amazing interior of modern Il Vicolo Residence Apart-hotel. When decorating its four rooms, designers took into account the most beautiful traditions of past centuries and harmoniously blended the latest fashion trends into the historical atmosphere. Each of the rooms includes pieces of antique furniture and fine carpets reflecting the traditions of past years. They stand in contrast to stylish modern furniture, original table lamps and drapery with fashionable fabrics. A carefully thought-out lighting system unites the bold design.

Some of the budget hotels in Verona also feature a unique design. Three comfortable rooms are available to travelers in Verona Design B&B. The rooms are decorated in white tones in a minimalist style, each one is furnished with an ultra-modern double bed. It is designed in such a way that there's a sense of floating in the air, and a built-in system of artistic illumination enhances it. Hotel guests will be able to choose a classic room with a square bed or a romantic room with a round bed. Spectacular artistic lighting makes the situation in the rooms truly unique.

Arte Nel Centro

From Verona center - 0.8 km

On the central street of Verona, you will find popular Arte Nel Centro Mini-Hotel, and the setting of its three charming rooms is a true work of design art. The ultramodern-style rooms are dominated by black and white colors with accessories of red shades complementing the decor. On the ground floor, there is a wonderful breakfast room furnished with priceless antique furnishings, which is striking with its exquisite natural-wood finish. A large collection of works of art and antiques is stored within the hotel walls.

Luxury accommodation

Top places to stay in Verona - most luxury and fashionable hotels

Palazzo Victoria

From Verona center - 0.2 km

One of the most luxurious hotels in Verona is Palazzo Victoria. Filled with an atmosphere of luxury and elegance, it occupies an outstanding historic building near the Juliet's House and magnificent Castelvecchio Castle. Luxurious rooms of the hotel are equipped with unique handmade furniture and priceless artworks, while in the public areas it was possible to restore old marble floors and finishing of rare wood species. The hotel runs its own national restaurant offering a rich menu and an impeccable wine list, as well as part of tables served in a glazed patio.

Hotel Accademia

From Verona center - 0.3 km

Another outstanding historic building in the city center is occupied by Hotel Accademia. Its wealthiest guests are offered accommodation in several exclusive rooms featuring antique wooden beams and a harmonious design. One of the main advantages of the hotel is a restaurant inviting visitors to taste the most popular dishes and wines of the Veneto region within its walls. All the culinary masterpieces are prepared exclusively from local products; the solemnly decorated restaurant is perfect for holding a banquet.

Grand Hotel Verona

From Verona center - 0.9 km

Upscale hotels worth noting include Grand Hotel Veronathat has prepared several luxury suites for high-status guests. The elite rooms are distinguished by a romantic design; a colonial-style bed and views of a wonderful Zen garden from the windows can also be found here. The rooms also feature high-class technical equipment: apart from the climate control system, they also include an iPod docking station. A garden surrounding the hotel is incredibly beautiful and harmonious. Terraces with sun beds and garden furniture can be found here in the warm season.

Hotel San Pietro

From Verona center - 15.6 km

A very spectacular modern building houses Hotel San Pietro, which is in walking distance from the business center of Veronafiere. The hotel is decorated in an elegant modern style, offering a huge selection of outdoor lounges and recreation areas in addition to inviting rooms. Connoisseurs of elite alcohol will definitely like an aristocratic bar, and those having a sweet tooth will be impressed by a cozy cafe with a huge selection of bakery products.

Hotel Fiera

From Verona center - 2.4 km

Cozy Hotel Fiera never disappoints travelers who prefer staying in a luxurious setting. Its guests can book several luxurious executive rooms. Each of these rooms has large panoramic windows and a spacious bathroom. The walls are finished with natural materials. Beautiful woodwork and chic parquet floor make the interiors very natural and attractive; the modern hotel perfectly suits both romantic couples and business tourists who are visiting Verona for business.

Crowne Plaza Verona Fiera

From Verona center - 3.6 km

A very original and remarkable place is top-rated Crowne Plaza Verona Fiera. Housed in a high-rise modern building with an extraordinarily decorated facade, the hotel has many unique and attractive features. On one of its last floors, there is a chic swimming pool with a hot tub, an artificial waterfall, and panoramic glazing. Business guests of the hotel will be surprised by the non-standard design of a conference hall, which is richly adorned with live plants. Gourmets will appreciate the menu of Plaza restaurant representing the national cuisine in its modern interpretation. The design of hotel rooms is also special - they are all generously decorated with chic designer furniture and rich fabrics.

Hotels With History

Preserved history of Verona: long-standing and historical hotels
Palazzo Maffei

From Verona center - 0.5 km

Verona is a treasure trove of unique historic hotels, some of which are known far beyond Italy. In the heart of the city, you will find Palazzo Maffei Aparthotel opened in a restored 17th-century building. The building has managed to retain its old stone spiral staircase and original high ceilings, tall narrow windows and part of sculptures, which presently adorn corridors of the hotel. Everywhere in the hotel, you can see priceless works of art, including a collection of old paintings and sculptures, as well as ceilings decorated with frescoes.

Hotel Colomba dOro

From Verona center - 0.1 km

A true embodiment of the culture of past centuries is Hotel Colomba dOro, which is just a couple of minutes walk from the Verona Arena. It occupies a unique building of a medieval monastery where a chic finish of stone and wood, as well as wonderful frescoes, have been restored during the reconstruction. Luxurious rooms are decorated taking into account the good old traditions - they have huge wooden beds with carved backs and antique furniture, while the drapery is made with satin and velvet. Special attention should be paid to a richly decorated breakfast room where pristine stone walls and elaborate mosaics are surprisingly well preserved.

B&B Palazzo Camozzini

From Verona center - 0.9 km

B&B Palazzo Camozzini can also be found in the central district of Verona. This budget hotel occupies an amazing 16th-century building. Behind its front door, there is a spacious hall decorated with antique furniture, carpets, and a huge crystal chandelier illuminating it. Only two cozy rooms with huge windows and a unique design made up of antiques are available for guests. Clients of the hotel will have an opportunity to get acquainted not only with the cultural but also with gastronomic traditions of Verona as well. Every morning they are served breakfast with a large selection of local delicacies.

Residenza Roccamaggiore

From Verona center - 0.9 km

An invaluable hotel from a historical point of view is Residenza Roccamaggiore. Its customers have a chance to spend a few days in one of the two fully equipped suites decorated with pristine frescoes and precious wood finishes. The apartments are furnished with restored antique items made of dark wood; among other interior items, you can notice a lot of interesting antique accessories. Old tableware, elegant vases with fresh flowers, wooden handicrafts, and lamps help recreate the atmosphere of the old days in all rooms.

The former Benedictine monastery building houses the Il Relais dell Abbazia, and each of its three rooms is unique. Stone masonry and massive wooden ceilings are restored inside, as well as incredibly beautiful antique furniture in a romantic style used for their decoration. A luxurious high-back bed decorated with handmade carvings, old paintings in massive wooden frames, bouquets of fresh flowers and beautiful drapery with light fabrics are the main interior elements of each room.

The Gentleman of Verona

From Verona center - 0.3 km

A building occupied by The Gentleman of Verona Hotel was built more than 400 years ago. Five luxury suites are equipped within its walls especially for fans of historic interiors. Apart from the abundance of antiques, they are particularly noteworthy for their chic finishes; high ceilings adorned with elaborate stucco and murals have been preserved inside. The rooms are perfectly illuminated by crystal chandeliers, and a mood of romance and aristocratic refinement is given by magnificent paintings and bouquets of fresh flowers.

Legendary Hotels

Verona legends. Famous hotels glorified by history or celebrities

Due Torri Hotel

From Verona center - 0.7 km

Upscale Due Torri Hotel has remained the most famous and symbolic hotel in Verona for many years. It has long been granted the status of an outstanding city landmark; the hotel is in the immediate vicinity of the Church of St. Anastasia and occupies a unique 14th-century building. One of the main features of the hotel is its luxurious interior striking with the abundance and variety of antiques. Pieces of antique furniture and artistic masterpieces can be seen not only in its public areas but also in the rooms; the hotel carefully preserves the refined and aristocratic atmosphere of past centuries.

In addition to luxury suites, the hotel has another attractive characteristic - a rich history full of remarkable events. Among the hotel's famous guests Goethe and Mozart, as well as Louis XVII of France who stayed at the hotel during the exile. This is where its secret coronation took place, which was only known to a narrow circle of people. The luxurious hotel is still popular among world celebrities. Thus, Versace and

Robbie Williams, Joe Cocker and Anthony Hopkins, Sophia Loren and George Michael, as well as Oasis band musicians stayed within its walls.

Il Sogno di Giulietta

From Verona center - 0.5 km

No less symbolic and interesting is five-star Il Sogno di Giulietta Hotel. The top-class hotel is primarily notable for its location, as it stands in the Juliet's Courtyard - one of the most iconic attractions of Verona. This particular courtyard was described by William Shakespeare in his tragedy. Il Sogno di Giulietta is considered an ideal hotel for a romantic stay in Verona. Its unique double rooms are individually decorated with priceless antique furnishings, rich fabrics, and works of art. Separate rooms offer a wonderful view of Juliet's Courtyard; guests will also have a chance to book one of the rooms including a panoramic balcony. Another secret kept by Il Sogno di Giulietta Hotel is the access to the famous courtyard in the evening hours when it is closed to the public.

Hotel Villa del Quar

From Verona center - 7.7 km

A unique place is Hotel Villa del Quar surrounded by beautiful vineyards located at a considerable distance from the bustling center of Verona. It can safely claim the title of one of the oldest hotels in the world - according to historical data, the first inn appeared on its site in the days of Ancient Rome. It hosted guests until the 16th century, and during the Middle Ages, it was decided to completely rebuild the historic hotel. The hotel's latest major reconstruction took place at the end of the 20th century when its interior was decorated with priceless antique furniture and artworks by outstanding Italian masters. Visitors to Verona will have a real opportunity to spend a few days in one of the oldest hotels on the globe.

Byblos Art Hotel Villa Amista

From Verona center - 9.1 km

Travelers who prefer to stay in the catchiest designer hotels should pay attention to prestigious Byblos Art Hotel Villa Amista. Its present location is a wonderful 15th-century villa, the interiors of which were designed by Alessandro Mendini, one of the most outstanding designers of the 20th century. A riot of colors and their unexpected combinations, elegant soft furniture of rich shades and a variety of author's accessories in a romantic style - the luxurious hotel's situation resembles the one typical of an original art gallery. Each and every element of this amazing hotel's interior is thought through to the smallest detail and is a true embodiment of the outstanding designer's talent.

Legendary hotels

Verona for couples in love - best hotels for intimate escape, wedding or honeymoon
Hotel Mastino

From Verona center - 0.4 km

Shrouded in legends about Romeo and Juliet, Verona will be an ideal place for romantic holidays in Italy. Within walking distance of Arena di Verona is Hotel Mastino offering couples a broad selection of individually furnished rooms. Some rooms are in cream shades and decorated with beautiful antique furniture, while others have a kind of canopy over a bed. Hotel guests are provided with a wide range of extra services; they can visit the nearby partner hotel's health-improving center or stroll through a well-kept garden in the evening.

Hotel Antica Porta Leona

From Verona center - 0.6 km

Prestigious Hotel Antica Porta Leona invites tourists to organize an unforgettable stay in a romantic setting. Several of its rooms are designed specifically for honeymooners, they feature a huge colonial-style bed with a translucent white canopy. The hotel was opened in a restored 15th-century building. In a hall with a vaulted ceiling on the ground floor, there is a very beautiful swimming pool. In addition, guests can enjoy a great wellness center with massage parlors, a sauna, and hot tubs.

Art&Breakfast

From Verona center - 9.1 km

A wonderful place to relax together is Art&Breakfast Mini-Hotel. Each of its three suites is decorated with unique works of art and antique accessories in a unique romantic style. The main attribute of all the suites is a huge bed in the style of past years dressed with rich linens. Antique furnishings and a dark-wood finish give the interior an aristocratic charm, while magnificent landscape paintings, crystal chandeliers, and fresh flowers help you tune in to a romantic mood.

Hotel Marco Polo

From Verona center - 0.5 km

Travelers who are not indifferent to the modern style would likely give preference to Hotel Marco Polo. Its romantic rooms are decorated with a predominance of white and cream colors, being complemented by very interesting designer furnishings and an adjustable lighting system.

Very cozy romantic rooms with massive wooden ceilings are located on the top floor and distinguished by a beautiful drapery with light fabrics. The pride of the hotel is its wellness center with spectacularly illuminated massage rooms and a relaxation area including a hot tub.

Le Suite Di Giulietta

From Verona center - 0.5 km

A synonym for romance is Le Suite Di Giulietta. This miniature hotel is ready to present its only 2 unique eco-friendly suites offering an amazing view of Juliet's balcony. The interior of the rooms is a harmonious combination of traditions of different epochs. Here you can see both genuine antiques and ultramodern decorations. Each suite has an open-plan bathroom, as well as windows and balconies overlooking Verona's most famous landmark - Juliet's balcony. Romantic Le Suite Di Giulietta has the status of an ecological hotel, being equipped with special energy-saving systems.

An excellent place for enjoying each other's company is Affittacamere Boutique Room. Each of the hotel's six charming rooms is decorated with exquisite designer furniture. The culture of past centuries is reflected in original beams under the ceiling. The beautiful decoration with beige and pearly fabrics helps make the atmosphere in the rooms especially romantic. To diversify their secluded stay at the hotel, guests can visit a luxurious spa with a lot of free services available. They can enjoy water treatments in a pool and a jacuzzi, relax in a salt cave or book a massage.

Shopping in Verona

Authentic goods, best outlets, malls and boutiques

Start your shopping in Verona with attendance of popular shopping centers. Over a hundred customized stores presents La Grande Mela shopping complex. Clothes and shoes of various price categories, original accessories and perfumes are available to customers. Shopping pavilions and restaurants are located on the first two floors. The third floor is entirely given up to recreational areas. There are many attractions and playgrounds for children, as well as a modern cinema and billiards.

Franciacorta Outlet Village is just ideal for enjoying shopping and money-saving. It houses over 160 stores. Shopping here will appeal to those who love LEVIS, Tomy Hilfiger and Calvin Klein brands. The presented clothing is of the highest quality and can be purchased at a discount of up to 70%. In the outlet, there are some large sportswear departments, perfumery and accessories stores.

Fashion District Mantova Outlet is an equally attractive place for shopping for frugal buyers. This outlet is one of the most popular in the city since all-year-round they sell quality brand items with a discount of up to 80%. It presents trade pavilions for visitors of different ages. Young people and older customers can choose the best things for themselves.

Grand'Affi Shopping mall continues to be a focus of Verona's guests' attention. It is one of the smallest in the city and includes only 40 shops. However, the variety of goods is simply amazing. There you'll find excellent leather goods, inexpensive footwear, and souvenirs. Ladies will be pleased with cosmetics and jewelry shops. Since its opening, the shopping center is a permanent venue for exhibitions and other entertainment events.

Excellent shopping is possible in the nine-story department store Upim. It is strikingly different from many other malls of the city. There are no stores of famous brands here. All the pavilions presented are notable for affordable prices, the quality of goods in them deserves the highest praise. This department store employs one of the city's largest souvenir shops, and there is also a large store with men's and women's bags.

Mazzi Overwear Outlet Store is extremely popular among women. You can buy luxurious fur coats and other garments made from natural fur with great discounts all-year-round. All things are of high quality, both in classical and modern styles.

There are several wonderful markets in Verona. One of the most popular is located in Piazza San Zeno square. This is one of the most colorful antiquities markets in Italy, where one can find many unique things. Many come here in search of old paintings and jewelry, others are attracted by antique pocket watches, books, and household decorations. In this market, for a modest fee, you can purchase very unusual souvenirs.

The city has several excellent shopping streets, one of the most fascinating is Via Mazzini. This is a narrow shady street, on both sides of which are designer shops with clothes and accessories, souvenir shops and stores that sell local delicacies and Italian wine. There are always a lot of people here, so morning is the best time for a comfortable walk.

One of the most luxurious and expensive shopping streets in Verona is Corso Santa Anastasia. It features trade pavilions of world-famous couturiers and Italian designers. On this street, there are several elegant antique shops, as well as shopping pavilions with special household decorations. Only the wealthiest tourists can afford to shop here

Quick Travel Guide to Verona

To Get in

By plane

Verona-Villafranca Airport (IATA: VRN) (ICAO: LIPX), named after the poet Valerius Catullus and thus also referred to as Verona 'Catullo' Airport, is the closest airport to Verona. It is located 12 km southwest of the city.

A shuttle bus service (the "Catullo airport service" operated by ATV) connect Verona's main railway station, Verona Porta Nuova to Verona-Villafranca Airport. A single journey costs €6 and travel time is 15-20 minutes. The service runs from 6 am to 11 pm every day with a frequency of 15 minutes during daytime hours. Tickets can be bought from machines at the airport's bus stop, which is outside the Arrivals Terminal, or directly from the bus driver.

Budget airlines fly from Brussels (Charleroi), Dublin, London-Gatwick, London-Stansted, Paris-Beauvais, Madrid, Alghero, Palermo, Trapani and Brindisi to Catullo Airport (IATA: VRN) of Verona.

National carriers fly from Frankfurt, Munich, London-Gatwick, Paris Charles de Gaulle, Rome-Fiumicino ('Leonardo da Vinci') and Moscow.

Alternative airports to Verona Villafranca are Venice 'Marco Polo' Airport or Treviso Sant'Angelo Airport.

By car

Although Verona Airport is located next to the junction of two motorways, the north-south A22 (Modena-Brennero and continues into Austria) and the east-west A4 (Milan-Venice), the access road to the Airport is located on Dossobuono's SS62 road, which can be accessed by leaving the A22 north of the A4-A22 Junction.

Rental car companies have stations at Verona-Villafranca Airport.

By train

Verona Porta Nuova station is served by regional, high-speed and international services. Trenitalia train services operate to destinations within Italy, such as Milan (Milano Centrale), Venice (Venezia Mestre and Venezia S. Lucia), Turin (Torino Porta Nuova and Torion Porta Susa), Bologna (Bologna Centrale), Florence (Firenze S. Maria Novella),

Rome (Roma Termini), Trieste (Trieste Centrale) and Bolzano (Bozen).

International services by ÖBB (Austrian Federal Railways), DB (Germany's Deutsche Bahn), SBB-CFF-FFS (Swiss Federal Railways) and Thello (Italy's and France's Trenitalia-SNCF night train) operate at Verona Porta Nuova to Vienna (Wien Miedling and Wien West), Munich (München Hbf and München Ost), Innsbruck (Innsbruck Hbf), Geneva (Geneve/Genf), Dijon and Paris (Paris Gare d'Est).

Luxury tourist train, the Venice-Simplon Oriental Express, operates between Venice and London (London Victoria) via Verona Porta Nuova, Innsbruck and Paris Gare d'Est).

Travel Time

1 hour 22 mins from Milan (Milano Centrale) by EuroCity or high-speed Freccia trains , or 1 hour 50 mins by Trenitalia RV (Regionale Veloce)

1 hour 10 mins from Venice (Venezia Santa Lucia) by EuroCity or high-speed Freccia trains , or 1 hour 22 mins by Trenitalia RV (Regionale Veloce) , also 2 hours 10 mins by Trenitalia R (Regionale)

49 mins from Bologna (Bologna Centrale) by high-speed Freccia or 1 hour 28 mins by Trenitalia RV (Regionale Veloce)

5 hours 20 mins from Munich (München Hbf) by EuroCity .

Trenitalia regional (R) trains also call at a smaller station, Verona Porta Vescovo, to the east of Verona Porta Nuova.

To Get around

Upon arrival at Verona Porta Nuova station, it is 15 minute walk down a long boulevard to reach the centre of town, the Verona Arena (Arena di Verona). Just leave the railway station, walk through the bus station and past a triumphal arch and follow the boulevard Corso Porta Nuova till the end.

Bus

Bus services in Verona are operated by ATV . The site has English version and up-to-date timetable and ticket information. As of 2014, a single 'urban' ticket (valid for 90 minutes on as many bus connections within Verona's central area) costs €1.30 from ATV's ticket office or any newsagent stores at Verona Porta Nuova station. Buying directly from the bus driver costs €2.00. You can also buy a bus ticket from one of several parking ticket machines scattered around town for €1.10.

Buses 11, 12 or 13 runs (among others) frequently rus between Verona Porta Nuova and the Verona Arena (bus stop: Piazza Bra). Journey time is 10 minutes. Busses 21, 22, 23, 24 and 61 travel from Porta Nuova to Castelvecchio and Porta Borsari.

Bike

Verona has a city bike hire scheme. It has a registration cost of €30 annually, €5 weekly or €2 daily, and is free for 30 minutes, then costs 50c, then 75c for each successive 30 minutes up to one hour, after which the rate goes up.

The End

Manufactured by Amazon.ca
Bolton, ON

32727916R00106